THE SPIRITUALITY OF MOTHER TERESA

Raniero Cantalamessa, OFM, Cap

Translated by Marsha Daigle-Williamson, PhD

Published by The Word Among Us Press
7115 Guilford Drive, Suite 100
Frederick, Maryland 21704
wau.org

23 22 21 20 19   1 2 3 4 5

ISBN: 978-1-59325-366-0
eISBN: 978-1-59325-367-7

CONTENTS

INTRODUCTION

This book contains the meditations I delivered to the pontifical household during Advent in 2003, following Mother Teresa of Calcutta's beatification on October 19 of that year. At the time, her personal diary had not yet been published.[1] Since I had used several texts from that diary, graciously made available to me by the general postulator of the cause for her beatification, it seemed appropriate to wait until the official edition of her diary had been released before publishing my meditations.

Further, various factors prompted me to take up this material again and convinced me of the usefulness of offering it to a wider audience than the initial audience of the papal household. Mother Teresa's canonization by Pope Francis took place on September 4, 2016; 2017 marked the twentieth anniversary of her death; and for the first time, I had the opportunity to visit Albania—the country Mother Teresa considered her homeland—to preach a retreat to the clergy. She was born in Skopje, in modern Macedonia, but her mother was Albanian and Mother Teresa spoke Albanian as her native language.

Interestingly, Enver Hoxha, the head of state of Albania from 1944 to 1985, boasted that in his lifetime he had made Albania the first country in the world whose "state religion" was atheism. During his dictatorship, he never allowed Mother Teresa to visit her country. After the fall of communism in the country, the statue of Hoxha, like the statues of Stalin in other cities, was demolished. In their place, images or statues of Mother Teresa can be found at every turn throughout the country, and Tirana International Airport is named for her. This is a small confirmation of where true greatness was.

At the time I gave these meditations, Pope John Paul II, as many may recall, had been seriously ill and suffering for some time. (He died a little over a year later.) Yet he never missed attending the meditations in the Redemptoris Mater Chapel. That fact explains some of my comments about him that at first sight could seem to be celebrating him. Like Mother Teresa, his great friend, he too had already reached that state in which people's words no longer had any power to distract him from the truth, and there was therefore no longer any risk of harming his humility.

In addition to these four meditations to the papal household, I have included some of my other talks, given in different circumstances, that speak about the person and work of Mother Teresa, and these are new for this English edition. In that same year, 2003, I went to Calcutta to record two television programs of Gospel commentaries that were broadcast every Saturday evening on Channel One in Italy, Rai 1. These commentaries demonstrate the spirit and the courage of this great woman. I have also added a talk that I gave at the Vatican in 2000 to the families who had adopted children through the Missionary Sisters of Charity. Finally, in the appendix, the reader will find two homilies given, respectively, by Pope John Paul II for the beatification of Mother Teresa of Calcutta and by Pope Francis for her canonization.

The original Italian edition of the meditations I delivered to the pontifical household during Advent in 2003 had the subtitle *A Saint for Atheists and Spouses*, which seemed less significant for this enlarged English edition and has been omitted. With it, as I explain in one part of the book, I intended to point to the message that this saint's experiences of the silence of God and of desolation can apply to an entire category of atheists—those for whom atheism is not a point of pride but a cause of suffering. It also offers hope to the many married people who no longer experience the same attraction to their spouse and the gratification they had at the beginning of their marriage but who continue nevertheless to love him or her, and more deeply and gratuitously than before.

CHAPTER 1

Go from Your Country

The beatification of Mother Teresa of Calcutta on October 19, 2003, has made it clear for the world that there is only one true greatness in the world—holiness. With the crowd filling every corner of St. Peter's Square and the Via della Conciliazione as the image of Blessed Mother Teresa was displayed and the *Alleluia* was being sung by the Sistine Chapel Choir, this truth was clear. What other person in the world is honored this way—and by such a huge crowd, gathered not by someone's command, as often happens in the mass gatherings of totalitarian regimes, but spontaneously out of admiration and love for the person?

It was a confirmation of a theory espoused by the famous thinker Blaise Pascal. He wrote that there are three orders, or levels, of possible greatness in the world: the order of bodies in which people with extraordinary beauty or physical prowess excel; the order of intelligence or genius in which artists, writers, and scientists excel; and the order of holiness in which, after Christ and the Virgin, the saints excel.[2] Pascal wrote that an almost infinite distance separates the second order from the first, but an infinitely more infinite distance separates the third order from the second—the order of holiness from the order of genius. Similarly, according to a saying attriubuted to the musician Charles Gounod, "One drop of holiness is worth more than an ocean of genius." The glory of holiness does not end with time but lasts eternally.

A journalist asked Mother Teresa point-blank one day what she felt about the whole world considering her a saint. She responded, "Holiness is not the luxury of the few, but a simple duty for you and for me."[3] She was thinking especially of the necessity of the practical application of the requirements of the gospel in the face of the needs of the world. We can add that it is a necessity on the metaphysical level as well. We need to become saints to be ourselves and to fulfill the fundamental vocation of being in the image and likeness of God (see Genesis 1:26): "You shall be holy; for I the LORD your God am holy" (Leviticus 19:2).

In his apostolic letter *Novo Millennio Ineunte*, Pope John Paul II said, "All pastoral initiatives must be set in relation to *holiness.*" This holiness, he explained, is above all an objective *gift* procured by Christ through his redemptive death that we have received in Baptism. He added, however, "The gift in turn becomes a *task*, which must shape the whole of Christian life"[4] It has been said that "after the Middle Ages had gone farther and farther astray in emphasizing the concept of Christ as the prototype, Luther came along and emphasized the other side, that he is a gift and this gift is to be received by faith."[5] The same author who said this, the philosopher and Lutheran believer Søren Kierkegaard, added, "But now in our time it is clear that what must come to the fore is the concept of Christ as prototype," and this, he said, is needed lest the unilateral emphasis on faith become a fig leaf for the most unchristian omissions.[6]

On several occasions, I have focused on the holiness of Christ as a free gift to *appropriate* through faith. This time, prompted by the example of Mother Teresa, I would like to emphasize the holiness of Christ as a model to *imitate* in our lives. In this regard, Mother Teresa asserted on one occasion,

"The church of God needs saints today. . . . This imposes a great responsibility on us to fight against our own ego and love of comfort that would lead us to choose a comfortable and insignificant mediocrity." [7] She believed each of us could become a saint: "Holiness . . . is a simple duty," [8] and the path to that holiness is prayer.

1. The Source of Holiness

We can discover in Mother Teresa's life the act that usually initiates the undertaking of holiness, the "cornerstone" of the building. We discover, to our joy, that this act can occur at any stage of life. In other words, it is never too late to begin to become a saint. St. Teresa of Avila lived a fairly ordinary life for many years—not without compromises—when the change occurred that made her become the person we now know her to be.

The same thing happened in the life of her namesake Mother Teresa of Calcutta. Until the age of thirty-six, she was a member of the Sisters of Loreto, faithful to her vocation and dedicated to her work, of course, but there was nothing that would predict something extraordinary in her. It was during a train ride from Calcutta to Darjeeling for her annual spiritual retreat that something happened that changed her life. The mysterious voice of God addressed a clear invitation to her: Leave your order, your former life, and put yourself at my disposal for a work that I will show you. Among the Missionaries of Charity, this day—September 10, 1946—is recorded as "the Day of Inspiration."

Thanks to the documents that came to light during the process for beatification, we know the exact words Jesus spoke to her: "I want Indian Missionary Sisters of Charity—who would be My fire of love amongst the very poor—the sick—the dying—the little street children—the poor I want you to bring to Me. . . . Wilt thou refuse?"[9] Jesus also said, "There are convents with numbers of nuns caring for the rich and [well] to do people, but for My very poor there is absolutely none."[10]

This moment in Mother Teresa's life was a reiteration of Abraham's experience when God said to him one day, "Go from your country and your kindred and your father's house to the land that I will show you" (Genesis 12:1). The "Go" addressed to Abraham is different from the order given later to Lot to leave Sodom (see Genesis 19:15). There is no indication that Ur of the Chaldeans was a particularly corrupt environment and that Abraham could not have been saved by staying there. In his *Roman Triptych: Meditations*, Pope John Paul II reflects on Abraham's possible sentiments when facing this divine proposal: "Why must I leave this place? / Why do I have to abandon Ur of the Chaldees?"[11]

The same questions occurred, as we know, to Mother Teresa, and it caused her inner suffering. She confided to Archbishop Ferdinand Périer, SJ, "I have been and am very happy as a Loreto Nun.—To leave [...] what I love and expose myself to new labours and sufferings which will be great . . . and all because Jesus wants it."[12] Addressing Jesus, she said, "Why can't I be a perfect Loreto Nun . . . —why can't I be like everybody else?"[13] She also told him, "My own Jesus—what you ask is beyond me. . . . Go, Jesus, and find a more worthy soul, a more generous one."[14]

This too repeats a pattern in the Bible. Moses said, "Oh, my Lord, I am not eloquent, either heretofore or since you have spoken to your servant" (Exodus 4:10), and Jeremiah said, "I am only a youth" (Jeremiah 1:6). But God knows how to distinguish whether the objections of those he calls come from resistance to his will or instead from fear of being wrong and not up to the task. He is not, therefore, offended by their requests for explanations. He was not put off by Mary's question, "How can this be?" (Luke 1:34), whereas he rebuked Zechariah and made him mute for the same question (see Luke 1:18). Mary's question did not come from doubt but from a legitimate desire to know what she should do to cooperate with what God was asking of her.

In the end, Mother Teresa, like Mary, gave God her complete *fiat*, yes. She said it through the events that we are familiar with, and she said it with joy. The Greek word for the Latin *fiat* is *genoito*. Unfortunately, what gets lost in the translation is a very important nuance: *genoito* is in the optative mood (indicating a wish or a hope) rather than expressing a concession like *fiat*. *Fiat* merely expresses simple agreement or resignation to something that will happen; it is almost like saying, "If this cannot be done in any other way, then *fiat voluntas tua*—your will be done!" In contrast, Mary's *fiat* expresses a desire, an eagerness, a joy for the thing that is to happen. That is why it is called the "optative" mood. "God loves a cheerful giver" (2 Corinthians 9:7)—here is a saying Mother Teresa never tired of inculcating in her daughters, and she especially demonstrated that all her life through her smile.

2. The Pomegranate Seed

At this point it is clear what the fundamental act is, that "cornerstone" on which Mother Teresa's and every Christian's holiness is based. It is the response to a call; it is obedience to divine inspiration, evaluated and recognized as such. Simone Weil, who was not a saint but passionately admired holiness, speaks of "that consent which the soul gives to God almost without knowing it, and without admitting it to itself. This is as an infinitely small thing [like a pomegranate seed] among all the carnal inclinations of the soul, and nevertheless this decides its destiny for ever."[15]

All the great deeds of holiness in the Bible and the history of the Church rest on a "yes" said to God at the moment in which he personally reveals his will to someone. Scripture makes the whole history of the chosen people depend on the faith-obedience of Abraham: "By your descendants shall all the nations of the earth bless themselves, *because you have obeyed my voice*" (Genesis 22:18, emphasis added). God then made the beginning of the new and everlasting covenant depend on Mary's faith-obedience.

In his autobiography *Gift and Mystery*, John Paul II writes, "In the autumn of 1942 I made *my definitive decision* to enter the Cracow seminary."[16] His italics in the text imply several unstated reasons that can be intuited. This decision was preceded by a call: it was the decision to respond to an invitation, as is the case in every priestly vocation. We now know what God built on his *fiat*, his "Here I am; I am going" that he said in 1942.

I can imagine Mother Teresa's amazement and emotion at the twilight of her life when she would think back to that train ride. How much God was able to do through her small and painful "yes!" How grandiose was the plan he had in mind that she knew nothing about! I can imagine her at the end of her life singing in an astonished and emotional way, "My soul magnifies the Lord. . . . He who is mighty has done great things for me" (Luke 1:46, 49).

At the beginning of 2003, I was honored to be invited by the Missionaries of Charity to preach the Spiritual Exercises to them in preparation for their general chapter to be held in Calcutta. (In reality they were the ones who preached the exercises to me through their extraordinary poverty and incessant prayer.) I had the impression, right from our first meeting, that Mother Teresa's desire from heaven was that the first chapter to be celebrated after her death should be the occasion for a moving and choral *Magnificat* to God by her daughters—for what he had done through her life and was continuing to do through them. I simply conveyed this impression to those present, and later, after the chapter ended, the mother general, Sr. Nirmala, confided to me that this was in fact what happened at the general chapter held after the retreat.

In each of our lives, as in Mother Teresa's life, there is a call; otherwise we would not be here. Our "yes" was perhaps also a "yes" said in the dark without knowing where it would take us. Years later we should not be hesitant to acknowledge what God has been able to build on that small "yes" despite our resistance and infidelity, and we should also intone a moving and grateful "My soul magnifies the Lord" (Luke 1:46).

3. Divine Inspirations

Now we need to recall a maxim from the ancients about devotion to the saints: *Imitari non pigeat quod celebrare delectat*, "We should not be lazy in imitating what we are glad to celebrate."[17] Mother Teresa's story reminds us of one essential thing for our sanctification: the importance of obeying inspirations. This is not something we should practice just once in our lives. After the first decisive call from God, many other subtle invitations follow—what we call divine inspirations. Our spiritual progress depends on our docility to them.

We can easily understand why faithfulness to inspirations is the shortest and surest path to holiness. Holiness is not the work of human beings; it is not enough, therefore, to have a very clear plan for perfection and then bring it to pass progressively. There is no model of perfection that is identical for everyone. God does not mass-produce saints; he does not like cloning. Every saint is an unprecedented invention of the Holy Spirit. God can ask one saint for the opposite of what he asks another. What is there in common, if we consider recent times, between Josemaría Escrivá de Balaguer and Mother Teresa? And yet both are saints in the Church.

We do not know concretely at the beginning, then, what holiness God wants from each of us. Only God knows, and he gradually reveals it as the journey goes on. It follows that in order to attain holiness, human beings cannot limit themselves to following general rules that are the same for everybody. Each of us must understand what God is asking of us, and only of us. Think what would have happened if Joseph of Nazareth had limited himself to following the rules of holiness faithfully as they were then known, or if Mother Teresa had insisted on observing the canonical regulations in place for religious institutions!

What God wants that is different and specific to each of us can be discovered through the events of life, a word from Scripture, or the guidance of a spiritual director, but the principal and ordinary means are precisely inspirations of grace. These are interior promptings of the Spirit in the depth of our hearts through which God not only makes clear what he is asking but at the same time also communicates the necessary strength to accomplish it, if the person consents.

Divine inspirations have something in common with biblical inspiration, aside from the authority and weight that are of course essentially different. "God told Abraham . . ."; "The Lord spoke to Moses . . .": this speaking by the Lord was not, from the phenomenological point of view, something different from what happens with inspirations of grace. The voice of God, at Sinai as well, does not resound externally but within the heart in the form of clear promptings originating from the Holy Spirit. The Ten Commandments were not written by God's finger on tablets of stone but on the heart of Moses, who then inscribed them on tablets of stone. "Men moved by the Holy Spirit spoke from God" (2 Peter 1:21). The men were the ones who spoke but, moved by the Holy Spirit, they were repeating what they had heard in their hearts.

Every faithful response to an inspiration is rewarded by more frequent and stronger inspirations. It is as if the soul is in training to reach an always clearer perception of God's will and a greater capacity to perform it.

4. The Discernment of Spirits

The trickiest problem about inspirations has always been to discern which ones come from the Spirit of God and which ones come from the spirit of the world, our own passions, or the evil one.

The issue of discernment of spirits has undergone a notable evolution over the centuries. At the beginning it was thought of as a charism that functioned to discern which words, prayers, and prophecies spoken in an assembly came from the Spirit of God and which did not. Later it served primarily to discern *one's own* inspirations and to guide one's choices. The evolution was not arbitrary; it was in fact the same gift even though it was applied to different subject matters.

There are some criteria for discernment that we can call objective. In the area of doctrine, they are summarized by Paul in recognizing Christ as Lord: "No one speaking by the Spirit of God ever says 'Jesus be cursed!' and no one can say 'Jesus is Lord' except by the Holy Spirit" (1 Corinthians 12:3). For John, they are summarized by faith in Christ and his incarnation: "Beloved, do not believe every spirit, but test the spirits to see whether they are of God; for many false prophets have gone out into the world. By this you know the Spirit of God: every spirit which confesses that Jesus Christ has come in the flesh is of God, and every spirit which does not confess Jesus is not of God" (1 John 4:1-3).

In the moral arena, one fundamental criterion is the consistency of the Spirit of God with himself. He cannot request something that is contrary to God's will as expressed in Scripture, the teaching of the Church, and the duties of one's state in life. A divine inspiration will never lead someone to commit acts that the Church considers immoral, no matter how many specious arguments the flesh is able to suggest in these cases—for example, the argument that God is love, so everything that is done in the name of love is of God.

If a religious disobeys his or her superiors, even for a laudable reason, it is surely not by an inspiration of grace, because the first inspiration that God sends is specifically that of obeying. Mother Teresa waited patiently for the ecclesial authorities to recognize her inspiration before acting on it.

At times, however, these objective criteria are not enough, because the choice is not between good and evil but between one good and another good, and the question is discovering what God wants in a specific circumstance. It was primarily in response to this need that St. Ignatius of Loyola developed his teaching on discernment.

He invites us to observe the intentions (the "spirits") behind a particular choice and the reactions they elicit.[18] We know that what comes from the Spirit of God brings joy, peace, tranquility, gentleness, simplicity, and light. What comes from the evil spirit instead brings sadness, turmoil, agitation, disquiet, confusion, and darkness. The apostle Paul highlights this by contrasting the fruits of the flesh (enmity, discord, jealousy, dissension, divisions, envy) and the fruits of the Spirit that are instead love, joy, peace, etc. (see Galatians 5:19-23).

It is true that in practice things are more complex. An inspiration can come from God but can nevertheless cause great disturbance. But this is not due to the inspiration, which is gentle and peaceful like everything that comes from God; it is due rather to the resistance to the inspiration. Even a calm and peaceful river, if it encounters obstacles, can develop eddies and maelstroms. If the inspiration is welcomed, the heart will immediately experience a deep peace. God rewards every small victory in this area, making the soul feel his approval, which is the purest joy that exists in the world.

5. Letting Oneself Be Led by the Spirit

The concrete fruit of this meditation should be a renewed decision to place our trust in the inner guidance of the Holy Spirit for everything, like a kind of "spiritual direction." If receiving inspiration is important for every Christian, it is vital for those who have the task of governing the Church. Only in this way can the Spirit of Christ guide the Church through his human representatives. It is not necessary for all the passengers on a ship to be glued to the radio on board to receive signals about the route, the icebergs, and the weather conditions, but it is indispensable that those in charge do so. It was a "divine inspiration" that Pope John XXIII courageously accepted that led to the Second Vatican Council and, in more recent times, to so many other prophetic gestures.

It was this need for the guidance of the Holy Spirit that inspired the words of *Veni creator*: *Ductore sic te praevio vitemus omne noxium*: "If thou be our preventing Guide, / no evil can our steps betide." In his *Roman Triptych,* the Holy Father John Paul II echoes this idea when he puts this prayer in the mouth of those present at the moment of electing Peter's successor: "You who see all—point to him!"[19]

We all need to abandon ourselves to the interior Master who speaks to us in quiet words. Like good actors, we need to listen carefully, on important and minor occasions, to the voice of this hidden prompter, so that we can faithfully recite our part on the stage of life.

It is easier than one might think because he speaks to us within, he teaches us everything, and he instructs us about everything. John assures us, "The anointing which you received from him abides in you, and you have no need that any one should teach you; as his anointing teaches you about everything, and is true, and is no lie" (1 John 2:27). At times a simple glance within is enough—a movement in the heart, a moment of recollection and prayer.

With the words of a very famous liturgical prayer, let us ask God, through the intercession of Blessed (now Saint) Teresa of Calcutta, for the gift of recognizing and following our divine inspirations the way she followed hers.

Actiones nostras, quesumus Domine, aspirando preveni et adjuvando prosequere, ut cuncta nostra oratio et operatio a te semper incipiat et per te cepta finiatur.

Lord, may everything we do begin with your inspiration and continue with your saving help. Let our work always find its origin in you and through you reach completion. We ask this through Christ our Lord.[20]

CHAPTER 2

Though I Walk through the Valley of the Shadow

One day Francis of Assisi, alluding to the chivalrous poems and the *chansons de geste* that were being written in his time, exclaimed, "The Emperor Charles, Roland, and Oliver, all paladins and valiant knights who were mighty in battle, pursued the infidels even to death, sparing neither toil nor fatigue, and gained a memorable victory for themselves; and by way of conclusion these holy martyrs died fighting for the Faith of Christ. We see many today who would like to attribute honor and glory to themselves by being content with singing about the exploits of others."[21] In one of his *Admonitions*, he explained what he meant by those words: "We ought to be ashamed of ourselves; the saints endured [many things], but we who are servants of God try to win honor and glory by recounting and making known what they have done."[22] These words come back to my mind as a somber reminder right now as I give the second meditation on the holiness of Mother Teresa.

1. In the Darkness of Night

What happened after Mother Teresa said her "yes" to the divine inspiration that was calling her to leave everything and to put herself at the service of the poorest of the poor? The world has clearly seen what happened *around* her—the arrival of her first companions, the ecclesiastical approval, the rapid pace of developing her charitable works—but right up until her death, no one knew what was happening *inside* of her.

That has been revealed by her personal diaries and the letters to her spiritual director that are about to be published soon (and have now been published), but several excerpts are already known.[23] Some secular commentators are completely mistaken about the meaning of these writings, asserting that they now force people to revise their idea of the person and holiness of Mother Teresa. Someone has even drawn the conclusion that one can be a saint even without faith.

In reality, these intimate writings, far from diminishing the stature of Mother Teresa of Calcutta, increase it, placing her alongside the great mystics of Christianity. One of the most famous definitions of mysticism describes it as "experiencing divine things" (*pati divina*).[24] The original expression cannot quite be translated, but we can understand it to mean experiencing God along with suffering, living a divine passion (in the dual sense of sorrow and love that the word "passion," *pathos*, encompasses). We see this definition fully realized in Mother Teresa's experience. Let us see what it involves.

A priest who was close to Mother Teresa wrote, "With the beginning of her new life in the service of the poor, darkness came on her with oppressive power."[25] A few brief excerpts are enough to give us an idea of the intensity of the darkness in which she found herself:

> There is so much contradiction in my soul.—Such deep longing for God—so deep that it is painful—a suffering continual— and yet not wanted by God—repulsed—empty—no faith—no love—no zeal. . . . Heaven means nothing—to me it looks like an empty place.[26]

It is not difficult to recognize immediately in Mother Teresa's experience a classic case of what the scholars of mysticism, following St. John of the Cross, generally call "the dark night of the soul." Johannes Tauler (1300–1361) has a striking description of this stage of the spiritual life:

Once we are abandoned in such a way as to no longer have any consciousness of God, we fall into such anguish that we no longer know if we were ever on the right path, nor do we know if God exists or not, or if we ourselves are alive or dead. Therefore, a sorrow falls on us that is so strange that it seems that the whole world is oppressing us. We no longer have any experience or knowledge of God, and everything appears repugnant to us, so that we seem to be imprisoned between two walls.[27]

All that we know leads us to think that this darkness accompanied Mother Teresa until her death,[28] with a brief interval in 1958 when she was able to write jubilantly, "Today my soul is filled with love, with joy untold—with an unbroken union of love."[29] If from a certain point on she almost never speaks of it, it is not because her night was over but because she had now adapted herself to living in it. Not only did she accept it, but she also recognized the extraordinary grace it held for her. "I have come to love the darkness.—For I believe now that it is a part, a very, very small part of Jesus' darkness and pain on earth."[30]

The most fragrant flower of Mother Teresa's night was her silence about it. She was afraid, in talking about it, of drawing attention to herself. Even the people closest to her suspected nothing of her inner torment right up until the end. On her orders, her spiritual director was supposed to destroy her letters, and if some of them were saved it was because he had made copies, with her permission, for the Archbishop of Calcutta and future Cardinal Lawrence Trevor Picachy, SJ, which were found among his papers after his death. The archbishop, fortunately for us, had refused to comply with Mother Teresa's request to destroy them.

The most insidious danger for people during this dark night is to be aware that this is what is occurring—that is, to be convinced that they are experiencing something that the great mystics lived through before them and to think of themselves as being part of a circle of elect souls. Through God's grace, Mother Teresa avoided this risk, hiding her torment from everyone with a never-ending smile.

> The whole time smiling—Sisters & people pass such remarks.— They think my faith, trust & love are filling my very being. . . . Could they but know—and how my cheerfulness is the cloak by which I cover the emptiness & misery.[31]

According to one of the Desert Fathers, "The victory over all afflictions that befall you . . . is . . . to keep silence."[32] Mother Teresa put that into practice in a heroic way.

2. In the Ranks of the Great "Desolate Ones"

Mother Teresa is in "good company" in her desolation. I would like to mention two cases that most closely recall Mother Teresa's situation: one from a few centuries ago, St. Paul of the Cross (1694–1775), and one from her own time, St. Pio of Pietrelcina, whom she actually met in person. Paul of the Cross, after having begun to establish a new congregation, the Passionists, and having experienced the intoxication of union with God, also entered into a dark night of the soul, which lasted for forty years, until the end of his life. Someone has described him as "the prince of the great desolate ones."[33] If Mother Teresa had known about the following passage in one of his letters, she would have realized she was in good company, even if such "consolation" is generally precluded in the state in which she found herself:

> Ah! A soul that has experienced heavenly caresses and then finds it must for a time be deprived of [everything]; even more, to come to a place where, as it seems to the soul, it is abandoned by God; where it seems God no longer wants it, does not care for it, and God seems to be highly displeased with it; when it seems that everything it has done has been done badly—ah! I do not know how to explain myself the way I would want. It is enough to know . . . that this is almost a pain of the damned—I will say that—a pain which goes beyond every pain.[34]

At the time of the canonization of Padre Pio of Pietrelcina, several secular observers expressed the opinion that the holiness of the mystic from Gargano was an archaic holiness, different from that of Mother Teresa, the saint of charity, which would constitute a modern kind of holiness. Now we are discovering that Mother Teresa was also a mystic and that Padre Pio was a "saint of charity," as demonstrated by his establishment of the hospital Casa Sollievo della Sofferenze (Home for the Relief of Suffering).

The mistake is to contrast these two categories of Christian holiness—high contemplation and intensive action—which, on the contrary, we often see admirably united. St. Catherine of Genoa, considered to be at the summit of mysticism, was proclaimed the patroness of hospitals in Italy by Pope Pius XII because of her work and that of her disciples with the sick and the incurable. She closely resembles Mother Teresa in our day.

In a well-done article written for the occasion of her beatification, an Indian author characterized Mother Teresa as "a sister for Gandhi."[35] Many traits certainly unite these two great souls, the two *Mahatmas* ("great souls") of modern India, but it is even more accurate, I believe, to see in Mother Teresa "a sister for Padre Pio." They share not only the same veneration in the Church but also the same whirlwind of fame in public opinion throughout the world. One stands out primarily for corporal works of mercy and the other for spiritual works of mercy. But it was precisely Mother Teresa who reminded today's world that the worst poverty is not poverty in material things but poverty with respect to God, humanity, and love— the poverty, in brief, of sin.

The characteristic that makes these two saints most similar is perhaps precisely the long dark night in which they lived their whole lives. In one of his letters to his confessor, Padre Pio wrote, "I live in a perpetual night."[36] I will always remember the impression I had in San Giovanni Rotondo when I read the letter, displayed in a picture frame in the choir loft, in which Padre Pio described the stigmata to his spiritual director. He ended it with words from Psalm 38:1: "LORD, rebuke me not in your anger, / nor chasten me in your wrath!" He was convinced—and that conviction accompanied him to his death—that the stigmata were not a sign of predilection and acceptance on God's part but, on the contrary, a sign of just punishment for his sins. This is what opened my eyes to the mystical stature of my brother friar, who had been of little interest to me up to that time.

In addition to both of these souls having spent their lives in the dark, they were convinced that they were "deceiving" people. St. Gregory the Great describes the characteristic of superior human beings: "Despite the pain of their own affliction, they do not neglect being useful to others. While they patiently withstand the adversity that afflicts them, they still take thought to teach others what is needful, like some great doctors who, although afflicted themselves, forget their own wounds to cure others."[37] This characteristic shines forth to an eminent degree in the lives of Padre Pio and Mother Teresa. We only need to look at what they were capable of doing for others—despite their spiritual condition—in the confessional and at the bedside of the dying.

The night of the soul, far from demonstrating a lack of faith within Mother Teresa and in her fellow companions on the journey, represents a supreme degree of faith. Jesus' beatitude "Blessed are those who have not seen and yet believe" (John 20:29) applies to the mystics in a very special way.

3. Not Only Purification

But why does this strange phenomenon of the night of the soul that lasts practically one's whole life happen? There is something new here with respect to what the teachers in the past have experienced and explained, including St. John of the Cross. This dark night cannot be explained only by the traditional idea of passive purification—the so-called "purgative way" that prepares a person for the illuminative and unitive ways—precisely because this dark night occurs after these souls have already reached the highest levels of contemplation and mystical union with God. Mother Teresa, Padre Pio, and others were convinced that it was a question precisely of purification; they thought their "I" was particularly difficult to overcome if God was compelled to keep them in this state for such a long time.[38] But this was certainly not the explanation.

There is an even deeper reason that explains this night that extends throughout one's whole life: it is so that they "may share his sufferings" (Philippians 3:10) and that "in their flesh they complete what is lacking in Christ's afflictions for the sake of his body, that is, the Church" (Colossians 1:24). Jesus in Gethsemane was the first to experience for everyone the dark night of the soul, and he died in that state, judging by his cry from the cross, "My God, my God, why have you forsaken me?" (Matthew 27:46). In his apostolic letter *Novo Millennio Ineunte*, concerning the "the face of sorrow" of Christ, John Paul II wrote,

Faced with this mystery, we are greatly helped not only by theological investigation but also by that great heritage which is *the "lived theology" of the saints.* The saints offer us precious insights which enable us to understand more easily the intuition of faith, thanks to the special enlightenment which some of them have received from the Holy Spirit, or even through their personal experience of those terrible states of trial which the mystical tradition describes as the "dark night." Not infrequently the saints have undergone *something akin to Jesus' experience on the Cross* in the paradoxical blending of bliss and pain. (27)

The pope cites the experiences of St. Catherine of Siena and Thérèse of the Child Jesus, but I believe he was also secretly thinking of Teresa of Calcutta. It is difficult for me to imagine that Mother Teresa could have met one-on-one with her great friend Karol Wojtyla so many times without ever confiding to him something about her state, if for no other reason than to ask him to pray for her. We know, in any case, that Mother Teresa came to see her trial as a response to her desire to share the *Sitio*, "I thirst," of Jesus on the cross:

> If my pain and suffering—my darkness and separation gives You a drop of consolation—my own Jesus, do with me as You wish. . . . Imprint on my soul and life the sufferings of Your Heart. . . . I want to satiate Your Thirst with every single drop of blood that You can find in me. . . . Please do not take the trouble to return soon.—I am ready to wait for You for all eternity.[39]

It would be a serious mistake to think that the lives of these people involve only grim suffering. *Novo Millennio Ineunte*, as we heard, speaks of "the paradoxical blending of bliss and pain" (27). In the depth of their souls, these people enjoy a peace and a joy that are unknown to the rest of humanity, deriving from the certitude—stronger in them than doubt—of being in God's will. St. Catherine of Genoa compares the suffering of souls in that state to that of purgatory, where souls "suffer a torment that is so extreme" it can only be comparable to the suffering of hell, but in that suffering there is a "joy comparable to . . . the joy of the blessed in paradise."[40] The joy and serenity that emanated from Mother Teresa's face was not a mask but a reflection of her profound union with God.

She was the one who was "deceived" about herself, not the people who saw her.

The endless night of some modern saints also has, in my opinion, a "protective" purpose. It is the means invented by God for saints today who, like Padre Pio and Mother Teresa, constantly live and work under a media spotlight. It is like an asbestos suit for those who have to walk into a fire; it is like insulation that prevents an electric current from dispersing and causing a short circuit. St. Paul said, "To keep me from being too elated by the abundance of revelations, a thorn was given me in the flesh" (2 Corinthians 12:7). The thorn in the flesh of God's silence turned out to be highly effective for Mother Teresa: it preserved her from any headiness in the midst of all the talk about her throughout the world, even at the time of being awarded the Nobel Peace Prize. "The pain within is so great," she said, "that I really don't feel anything for all the publicity and the talk of the people."[41]

This attitude also links Mother Teresa to Padre Pio. One day, while looking out of the window at the crowd gathered in the square, Padre Pio asked his brother friar next to him, "But why have all these people come here?" And when he responded, "For you, Father," he quickly withdrew, sighing, "If only they knew . . ."

4. Alongside Atheists and Spouses

Rather than being "archaic" saints, the mystics are the most modern among the saints. Today's world has come to know a new category of people: atheists in good faith, those who experience God's silence painfully, who do not believe in God, but who do not boast about this. Instead they experience existential anguish and a lack of meaning in everything. They also, in their own way, live the dark night of the soul. In his novel *The Plague,* Albert Camus calls them "the saints without God."[42] The mystics exist above all for them; they are their companions on the journey and at the table. Like Jesus, they receive sinners and eat with them (see Luke 15:2).

This explains the passion with which certain atheists, once they were converted, steeped themselves in the writings of the mystics: Paul Claudel, Georges Bernanos, Jacques and Raïssa Maritain, Léon Bloy, the Swiss writer Joris-Karl Huysmans, and so many others delved into the writings of Angela of Foligno, and T. S. Eliot into the writings of Julian of Norwich. They found there the same landscape they had left, but now it was illuminated by the sun. Few people know that among the sources of inspiration for Samuel Beckett, the author of *Waiting for Godot,* were the works of St. John of the Cross.

The word "atheist" can have an active meaning and a passive meaning. It can indicate someone who rejects God but also someone who—at least it seems to that person—is rejected by God. In the first instance, it is a blameworthy atheism (if it is not in good faith). In the second instance, it is an atheism of sorrow or of atonement. In line with this second sense, we can say that mystics who are experiencing the dark night of the soul are literally a-theist, without-God. Mother Teresa wrote some things that no one would have suspected.

> They say people in hell suffer eternal pain because of the loss of God. . . . In my soul I feel just that terrible pain of loss— of God not wanting me—of God not being God—of God not really existing (Jesus, please forgive my blasphemies).[43]

The mystics are just a step away from the world in which people live without God; they have experienced the oppression of becoming dejected. Mother Teresa writes to her spiritual director, "I have been on the verge of saying—NO. . . . I feel as if something will break in me one day."[44] She also asks, "Pray for me that I may not refuse God in this hour.—I don't want to do it, but I am afraid I may do it.[45]

However, Mother Teresa was aware of the different nature of the solidarity and atonement of her "atheism." She writes, "I wish to live in this world which is so far from God, which has turned so much from the light of Jesus, to help them—to take upon myself something of their suffering."[46] She also believed that "If I ever become a saint—I will surely be one of 'darkness.' I will continually be absent from heaven—to light the light of those in darkness on earth."[47]

Because of this, mystics are the ideal evangelizers in the postmodern world, where people live *etsi Deus non daretur*, "as if there were no God." They can remind honest atheists that they are "not far from the kingdom of God" (Mark 12:34), that they would only need to take a leap forward to find themselves on the shores of the mystics, going from nothing to everything. Karl Rahner was correct when he said, "The Christian of the future will be a mystic or he will not exist at all."[48] Padre Pio and Mother Teresa are the answer to this sign of the times. We must not "waste" the saints by reducing them to being dispensers of grace or good examples.

However, mystics, in their dark night state, are also the living rebuttal to modern atheism, especially Marxist or Freudian atheism. That atheism is based on the ideas of projection or sublimation. Human beings project into heaven their unfulfilled desires on earth; they transfer their need for the protection and tenderness they experienced (or did not experience!) with their earthly fathers unto a good and welcoming heavenly Father. Religious people do everything in view of a reward. In contrast to that analysis, these mystic souls remain attached to a God who does not give or promise them anything, not even paradise, under a heaven that is closed. Who could give them the strength to do what they have done—to forget themselves, to think about others all the time, to clasp lepers, to embrace the dying—if not that Being who alone can operate without being seen because he is "more inward than our inmost selves"?[49]

I am convinced that the experience of the dark night by Mother Teresa and other mystics in general holds an important message for those in the married state as well. One time, in speaking to a group of women, she exhorted them to smile at their husbands. One of them objected, "Mother, you can say that because you're not married, and you don't know my husband." She answered, "I too am married, to Jesus, and I assure you at times it is not easy for me to smile at my spouse either."[50]

The process that leads to a successful marriage is like the process that leads to holiness in certain ways. The journey with a loved one in marriage, like that of the saints with God, includes the so-called "initial graces": the joy, tenderness, and attraction that make people seem to walk on clouds—things, however, that do not last forever. Then "the night of the senses" occurs for both of them, a state in which they have no feeling, no passion; things are dry and empty; they do everything through willpower and with effort, just out of sheer duty. At times this is followed by "the night of the soul," which is even worse because the crisis now involves not only feelings but also the mind and the will. They end up doubting if they are on the right path and if they may have been wrong about everything; complete darkness sets in.

But in both cases, whether in the relationship with a spouse or with God, all of this is not the end of everything but the prelude to a purer love. After getting past this crisis, saints become aware of how imperfect their initial love was, how much self-seeking was still involved in what they did; they loved God for the consolations they received and not just for himself. Spouses become aware as well of how their reciprocal attraction in the early days was so minor when compared to the real, genuine love that has matured because of the events in life they faced together. If at the beginning they loved each other for the satisfaction they each got, perhaps today they love each other a bit more for who each one is—that is, they love the other and not themselves. I am sure that many spouses would not find it difficult to recognize their own experience in what I am saying.

5. Our Minor Night

The mystics, however, have something to say to us believers today as well, and not just to atheists. They are not an exception or a category apart from other Christians. Instead, they demonstrate, by way of amplification, what the full expansion of the life of grace should be. We learn one thing above all from the dark night of the mystics and in particular that of Mother Teresa: how to conduct ourselves in times of dryness, when prayer becomes a struggle, an effort, like "beating our heads against a wall."

There is no need to focus on Mother Teresa's prayer during all the years she spent in darkness; the image of her at prayer is one we all still have in our minds. A series of beautiful prayers are among the most precious legacies she left her daughters and the Church. The Gospel writer Luke says about Jesus, "Being in an agony he prayed more earnestly," *factus in agonia prolixius orabat* (Luke 22:44). This is also what we observe in the lives of the mystics.

Dryness in prayer, when it is not the result of dissipation or compromises with the flesh but is allowed by God, is commonly the lesser form of the night of the soul for the majority of people who aspire to holiness. In this situation, it is important not to give up and begin to omit prayer in order to focus on activities, given the fatigue they find in prayer. When God is not there, it is important that at least his place stays empty and is not taken over by an idol, especially the idol of "activism."

To avoid this, it is good to interrupt work every so often and lift up one's thoughts to God or simply sacrifice a bit of time for him. In times of dryness, we need to discover a kind of special prayer that Blessed Angela of Foligno called "forced prayer" that she says she practiced:

> It is a good thing and very acceptable to God, my son, if you pray, keep vigils, and perform other good works when the fervor of divine grace is with you, but it is altogether most pleasing and acceptable to God that, when divine grace is lacking or has been withdrawn from you, you do not pray less, keep vigils less often, and perform fewer good works. Act without grace just as you do with grace. . . . Do your share, my son, and God will do his part well. Forced prayers, my son, are particularly pleasing to God.[51]

This is a prayer that we do more with the body than with the mind. There is a secret alliance between the will and the body. Often when our wills cannot command our minds to have or not have certain thoughts, we can command our bodies and tell our knees to bend, our hands to be folded, and our mouths to open and say a few words, for example, "Glory be to the Father and to the Son and to the Holy Spirit."

An Eastern mystic, Isaac the Syrian, said that when our hearts are cold and we can no longer utter even the smallest prayer or supplication, may the Lord find us continuously prostrate with our faces to the ground. Mother Teresa herself was also familiar with this "forced prayer":

> The other day, I can't tell you how badly I felt.—There was a moment when I nearly refused to accept [this state].—Deliberately I took the rosary and very slowly without even meditating or thinking—I said it slowly and calmly.[52]

Simply remaining physically in church, or in a place chosen for prayer, simply *being* in prayer, is then the only way left for us to continue to persevere in prayer. God knows we could go do a hundred more useful things that would be more gratifying for us, but we stay there and spend the time allotted in our schedule or in our initial resolve to the very end.

To a disciple who was continually lamenting not being able to pray because of distractions—"My thoughts trouble me," he said—the ancient monk to whom he was speaking told him to let his thoughts go wherever they wanted, "only do not leave your cell!"[53] This is good advice for us as well when we find ourselves having chronic distractions that are no longer in our power to control: let our thoughts wander where they will, but may our body remain at prayer!

In times of dryness, we need to remember the apostle's very encouraging word: "The Spirit helps us in our weakness" (Romans 8:26). Without our sensing it, he fills our words and sighs with a desire for God, with humility, with love. The Paraclete then becomes the strength of our "weak" prayer, the light of our dull prayer—in brief, he animates our prayer. Truly, as the Pentecost Sequence, the *Veni Sancte Spiritus*, says, he "waters what is dry," *rigat quod est aridum*.

All of this comes about by faith. It is enough for me to say, "Father, you have given me the Spirit of Jesus. Forming thereby 'one single spirit' with him, I recite this psalm, I celebrate this Mass, or I am simply silent here in your presence. I want to give you the very glory and joy Jesus would give you if he were the one still praying to you on earth." With this certitude let us conclude our reflection with this prayer:

Holy Spirit, you who intercede in the hearts of believers with sighs too deep for words, come help us in our weakness; knock at the hearts of the many of people who live without God and without hope in this world. Enlighten the minds of those who at this time are shaping the future of our planet. Help them understand that Christ is not a threat to anyone but a brother to all. For the poor, the lowly, the persecuted, and those excluded from the world of tomorrow, let not the assurance be taken away from them, in guilty silence, that until now has most defended them from the arbitrariness of the powerful and the harshness of life: the name of their brother, Jesus of Nazareth!

CHAPTER 3

Do You Really Know the Living Jesus?

1. Jesus, the Meaning of Mother Teresa's Life

Mother Teresa's confessor, the Jesuit Fr. Celeste Van Exem, said about her, "The meaning of her whole life was a person: Jesus."[54] The postulator for the cause of her beatification, Fr. Brian Kolodiejchuk, after having studied her life, her writings, and the testimonies of others about her for years, concluded, "If I have to say, in synthesis, why she is raised to the honor of the altar, I reply: because of her personal love of Jesus which she lived in such an intense way as to consider herself his bride. Hers was a Jesus-centered life."[55]

The most significant testimony in this regard is the letter that Mother Teresa wrote in Varanasi to the whole family of Missionaries of Charity during Holy Week on March 25, 1993. At the beginning, she wrote, "This letter being very personal, I wanted to write it in my own hand." She went on to say,

> I worry some of you still have not really met Jesus—one to one—you and Jesus alone. We may spend time in chapel—but have you seen with the eyes of your soul how he looks at you with love? Do you really know the living Jesus—not from books but from being with him in your heart? Have you heard the loving

words he speaks to you? . . . Never give up this daily intimate contact with Jesus as the real living person—not just the idea.[56]

Here we see that Jesus was not an abstraction for Mother Teresa—a set of doctrines and dogmas or the remembrance of a person who lived at another time, but a real, living Jesus, someone to gaze at in our heart and whom we allow to gaze at us.

Mother Teresa explains that if she had never spoken so openly until now, it was from a sense of reserve and in imitation of Mary, who "kept all these things in her heart" (Luke 2:19). However, now she felt the need before leaving them to explain the meaning of all her work: "For me it is so clear—everything in MC [Missionaries of Charity] exists only to satiate Jesus."[57]

To the question "Who is Jesus to me?" she responds with an inspired litany of titles:

Jesus is the Word—to be spoken. . . .
Jesus is the Life—to be lived.
Jesus is the Love—to be loved.
Jesus is the Joy—to be shared.
Jesus is the Sacrifice—to be offered.
Jesus is the Peace—to be given.
Jesus is the Bread of Life—to be eaten.[58]

Her love for Jesus spontaneously takes the form of a spousal love. She recounts the following:

Because I talk so much of giving with a smile, once a professor from the United States asked me: "Are you married?" And I said: "Yes, and I find it sometimes very difficult to smile at my spouse, Jesus, because He can be very demanding—sometimes."[59]

The majority of tall trees have a main root, called the tap-root, that descends perpendicularly into the ground and is like the continuation of the trunk under the ground. This is what gives some trees, like oaks, their sturdiness, so that not even the strongest winds can succeed in uprooting them. A human being also has a taproot. For a person who lives according to the flesh, it is one's "I," the disordered love of self—egotism; for the spiritual man, it is Christ. The whole path to holiness consists in changing the name and the nature of this root, to the point that one is able to say with the apostle, "It is no longer I who live, but Christ who lives in me" (Galatians 2:20). Thanks to the long duration of her dark night of the soul, which she considered as purification, Mother Teresa carried to completion this process in which we are all engaged.

2. The Fruit of Love Is Service

One of the most well-known sayings of Mother Teresa is "The fruit of love is service, / The fruit of service is peace."[60] These two things—love for Jesus and service to the poorest of the poor—poured forth together like a torrent of lava into Mother Teresa's soul at the moment of her second calling on September 10, 1946. She said to her daughters,

> "I Thirst" and "You did it to me"—Remember always to connect the two, the means with the Aim. What God has joined together let no one split apart. . . . Our charism is to satiate the thirst of Jesus for love and souls—by working at the salvation and sanctification of the poorest of the poor.[61]

"You-did-it-to-me": Mother Teresa marked out each of these words on the fingers of her hand and said they comprised "the Gospel in our five fingers."[62] For Mother Teresa, Jesus, who is present in the Eucharist, is present in a different but equally real way "in the distressing disguise of the poor."[63] The litany in honor of Jesus recorded above continues without any break:

Jesus is the Hungry—to be fed.
Jesus is the Thirsty—to be satiated.
Jesus is the Naked—to be clothed.
Jesus is the Homeless—to be taken in.
Jesus is the Sick—to be healed.
Jesus is the Lonely—to be loved.[64]

We all know how far the levels of her service to the poorest of the poor went. At one meeting a nun remarked to her that she was pampering the poor and offending their dignity by giving them everything free without asking anything of them. Mother Teresa responded, "There are so many congregations that pamper the rich that it's not bad if there is one who pampers the poor."[65] The head of social services in Calcutta had understood better than anyone else, according to Mother Teresa, the spirit of her service to the poor. One day he said to her, "Mother Teresa, you and we are doing [the] same social work. But there is a great difference between you and us. We do it for something, and you do it for somebody."[66]

Some have seen this as a limitation, not an asset, of Christian love for one's neighbor. But doesn't loving one's neighbor "for Somebody," for Jesus, mean not exploiting one's neighbor or diminishing him or her for a different purpose that, at its worst, can be egotistical in earning merit for heaven?

This might be true in every other case, but not when it is a question of Jesus, because it is contrary to the dignity of the human being to be subordinated to another creature but not contrary to his or her dignity to be subordinated to the Creator himself, God. In Christianity there is an even stronger reason: Christ identified himself with the poor. The poor person and Christ are one and the same: "You did it to *me*" (Matthew 25:40, emphasis added). To love the poor out of love for Christ does not mean loving them "through a third party" but *in person*. This is the mystery that is imprinted on Mother Teresa's life and of which she prophetically reminded the Church.

Love for Jesus prompted Mother Teresa, like other saints before her, to do things that no other motive in the world—political, economic, or humanitarian—would have been able to induce her to do. One time someone, observing what Mother Teresa was doing for a poor person, exclaimed, "I would not do that for all the gold in the world!" Mother Teresa replied, "Neither would I!" She meant, of course, that she would not do it for all the money in the world but would do it for Jesus.

Mother Teresa knew how to give the poor not just bread, clothes, and medicine but what they had even more need of: love, human warmth, dignity. In her speech in Washington during the National Prayer Breakfast on February 3, 1994, she emotionally recalled the time a man was found half-eaten by maggots in a garbage dump. After she brought him home and treated him, he said, "I have lived like an animal in the street, but I am going to die as an angel, loved and cared for." He died shortly after, saying with a big smile, "Sister, I am going home to God."[67] Mother Teresa, holding an abandoned baby in her arms or bending over a dying person, is, I believe, the very icon of God's tenderness.

3. "I Am among You as One Who Serves."

And now the question of application: What is this aspect of Mother Teresa's life saying to us? She reminds us that true greatness among human beings is not measured by the power that we exercise but by the service we give: "Whoever would be great among you must be your servant" (Matthew 20:26).

No one is exempt from some kind of service to the poor, but that service can take on different forms because people's needs are many and diverse. Paul speaks of "the service of the Spirit," *diakonia Pneumatos* (2 Corinthians 3:8) with which the ministers of the new covenant are charged. In Acts of the Apostles, Peter speaks of the apostles' "ministry of the word," which is more important than "serving tables" (Acts 6:2-4). The exercise of authority and ecclesial magisterium is also part of this service. Jesus said to his apostles, "I am among you as one who serves" (Luke 22:27), and in what did that service consist if not in teaching them, correcting them, and preparing them for their future mission?

What Mother Teresa reminds all of us is that for any Christian service to be genuine, it must be motivated by love for Christ. Paul said to the Corinthians, we are "your *servants for Jesus' sake*" (2 Corinthians 4:5, emphasis added). It is also possible for whoever works in the Curia to put into practice what Mother Teresa called "the gospel in our five fingers"— five words: You did it to me. It means doing everything, even bureaucratic procedures, for Jesus, seeing Jesus in those we are called to serve.

On this occasion, as the preacher to the papal household, I feel the need to leave behind the persuasive tone of "things we should do" and to assume instead a joyful tone of thanksgiving for what already is. I cannot let the opportunity here pass without uniting my small voice to that of the whole Church. For twenty-five years we have seen a man who has worn himself out in "the service of the Spirit." With respect to John Paul II, the title *Servus servorum Dei*, "the servant of the servants of God," introduced by St. Gregory the Great, is not just one title among many but the summary of a life.

His service, like that of Mother Teresa, has also had its source in love for Jesus. How many times has the Holy Father repeated the phrase from the Gospel that depicts Peter's pastoral service as an expression of love for Christ? Simon, son of John, do you love me? Tend my sheep (see John 21:15). It is a sign that this word has been the motivating inspiration for his pontificate and is what still impels him to give himself for the Church. Mother Teresa often said, "Love, to be real, must cost—it must hurt."[68] And one cannot in fact say that suffering has been absent all these years in the life of Peter's successor.

Nor has a tenderness been absent that is reminiscent of Mother Teresa. We were moved the other evening in Montecitorio Palace to see many instances of this in the first showing of the documentary *John Paul II: Witness of the Invisible*. Among the most striking images are those in which the pope hugs and kisses children or sick people. These images made me think of the word of God in Hosea: "I became to them as one / who raises an infant to his cheeks" (Hosea 11:4).

Your Holiness—there is a passage in the New Testament that seems written for you to deliver to the whole Church, so allow me to read it, for our sake more than for yours. The Letter to the Romans speaks of "the encouragement of the Scriptures" that helps us to "have hope" (Romans 15:4). I believe that conveying some of that encouragement from Scripture is the only thing that justifies the office that I have held for twenty-four years. The passage in question is Paul's farewell address to the Church of Ephesus:

> You yourselves know how I lived among you all the time . . . , serving the Lord with all humility and with tears and with trials. . . . I did not shrink from declaring to you anything that was profitable, and teaching you. . . . But I do not account my life of any value nor as precious to myself, if only I may accomplish my course and the ministry which I received from the Lord Jesus, to testify to the gospel of the grace of God. . . . I did not shrink from declaring to you the whole counsel of God. Take heed to yourselves and to all the flock, in which the Holy Spirit has made you guardians, to feed the Church of the Lord which he obtained with his own blood. . . . And now I commend you to God and to the word of his grace, which is able to build you up and to give you the inheritance among all those who are sanctified. (Acts 20:18-32)

Paul was mistaken on only one point that day, and this is reassuring to us. He said they would no longer see his face, which brought the people to tears. It caused apprehension, but it was not a prophecy. From the pastoral letters it seems that he did see the Church at Ephesus again two years later, at the end of his first imprisonment by the Romans (see 1 Timothy 1:3).

If I have been wrong to take the liberty of speaking this way, Holy Father, blame Mother Teresa, because she is the one who suggested that I do so with the love that this new Catherine of Siena had for Peter's successor.

4. The Love of Christ "of Which Nothing Greater Can Be Thought."

But now a conclusion for Christmas. Mother Teresa has reminded us today about the secret mainspring of her service to the poor and of her whole life: love of Jesus. And this is also the secret to a true Christmas celebration. In the Christmas carol *Adeste Fidelis*, there is a verse that says, "*Sic nos amantem quis non redamaret?*" "Who could not love him who loves us thus?" A loving heart is the only crib Christ wants to come to at Christmas.

But where do we find this love? Mother Teresa knew who to ask: Mary! One of her prayers says, "Mary, my dearest mother, Give me your heart so beautiful, so pure, so immaculate, so full of love and humility. That I may receive Jesus as you did. And go in haste to give him to others."[69]

We need to be even bolder than Mother Teresa on this point. Let me explain. Mother Teresa had a marvelous spirituality, which I have tried to highlight through some excerpts. But her spirituality, as well as Padre Pio's, is marked by the times in which both were formed. A clear trinitarian perspective was missing at that time in theological reflection (but not from their lives!), which now—since the Second Vatican Council, for example, in *Novo Millennio Ineunte*—seems to be the source and form of all Christian holiness. Her spirituality, as the postulator for her cause notes, was "Jesus-centered" more than Trinitarian.

Mother Teresa has different beautiful prayers to the Virgin but none to the Holy Spirit (at least in her writings that are known up to now). He is rarely named and almost always incidentally in the context of traditional liturgical formulas. There is no doubt that her holiness, like that of all the saints, is the work of the Holy Spirit from top to bottom. St. Bonaventure says about the wisdom of the saints, "No one receives it except him who desires it, and no one desires it except he who is penetrated to the marrow by the fire of the Holy Spirit."[70] However, this role of the Holy Spirit was not sufficiently highlighted in spiritual and theological formation in the past.

Fortunately, it is not the breadth of theological perspectives that makes saints but rather heroism in charity. Besides, no saint possesses by him or herself all the charisms or exhausts all the potential in the divine model of Christ. That fullness is found in the totality of saints as a group—that is, in the Church, not in the individual. The members of any religious institute would be very wise to preserve the legacy transmitted by the founder intact but at the same time remain open to receive the new light and new graces the Spirit never ceases to bestow on the Church.

It is perplexing to see movements or communities in which everything—every word of God, every spiritual insight and initiative—comes strictly from the leader or founder and is conveyed to his followers by him. It is as if people, as a result, were renouncing having their own personal relationship with God, within their common charism, to become mere relay stations.

What can we discover that is new about love for Jesus if we begin with a Trinitarian perspective? Something extraordinary: there exists a love for Jesus that is perfect, infinite, the only love worthy of him, the love "of which nothing greater can be thought."[71] And we discover that it is possible for us to participate in it, to make it ours, to welcome Jesus at Christmas with it. It is the love with which the heavenly Father loves his Son in the very act of generating him.

In Baptism we have received that love, because the love with which the Father loves his Son throughout eternity is called the Holy Spirit, and we have received the Holy Spirit. What else do we think is "God's love [that] has been poured into our hearts through the Holy Spirit" (Romans 5:5) if it is not literally the love of God—the eternal, uncreated love with which the Father loves the Son and from which every other love derives?

I said last time the mystics are not in a category apart from other Christians; they do not exist to astound us but to point out to all of us what the full development of the life of grace looks like in magnified form. And the mystics have taught us precisely this: that by grace, we have been inserted into the vortex of trinitarian life. St. John of the Cross says that God communicates to souls "the same love he communicates to the Son, though not naturally as to the Son, but . . . through unity and transformation of love. . . . The soul will participate in God himself by performing in him, in company with him, the work of the Most Blessed Trinity."[72]

Jesus himself assures us of this clearly when he prays to the Father "that the love with which you have loved me may be in them" (John 17:26). Through grace, the same love with which the Father loves the Son is therefore in us. What a discovery! What horizons for our prayer and contemplation! Christianity is grace, and this is what that grace is: participation in the divine nature (see 2 Peter 1:4)—that is, in divine love, since love is the very "nature" of the God of the Bible.

Some mystics, like Meister Eckhart, have spoken about a special, mysterious Christmas that occurs "in the very center of our souls"; it is celebrated when a person, with faith and humility, allows God the Father to give birth to his own Son anew in himself or herself.[73] A recurring maxim among the Fathers—from Origen to St. Augustine and St. Bernard—says, "What profit is it to you, if Christ once came in the flesh, unless he also comes into your soul?"[74] The custom of celebrating three Masses on Christmas day has traditionally been explained this way: the first commemorates Christ's eternal generation from the Father; the second, his historical birth from Mary; and the third, his mystical birth in the soul.

The German mystic Angelus Silesius expressed this idea in two verses: "Though Jesus Christ were born in Bethlehem a thousand times / but not in you, then you are lost forever."[75] The famous Italian convert Giovanni Papini was meditating on these verses during Christmas in 1955, and he asked himself how this interior birth could take place. The answer he gave himself—and it can serve us as well—was the following:

This new miracle is not impossible provided it is desired and expected. On the day you do not feel a hint of bitterness and jealousy before the joy of an enemy or a friend, rejoice because it is a sign that this birth is close by. . . . On the day you feel the need to bring a bit of happiness to someone who is sad and feel the impulse to relieve the pain or misery of even one creature, be glad because God's arrival is imminent. And if one day you are struck down and victimized by misfortune, and you lose your health, strength, children, and friends and have to endure indifference, malice, and coldness from those who are near and those far away, and despite all that, you do not abandon yourself to complaints and blasphemies and calmly accept your destiny, then exult and be triumphant because the miracle that seemed impossible has happened, and the Savior has now been born in your heart.[76]

All of these are "signs" of the birth that has taken place, but its cause, what produces it, is what Papini described at the beginning: desire and expectation. It is a faith full of expectation, certain of its coming—"expectant faith," according to a current Christian expression. Mary also conceived Christ in this way—in her heart, by faith—before she conceived him physically in her flesh: *prius concepit mente quam corpore.*[77]

We do not need to have any particular "feelings." (Who can "feel" a thing like this?) It is enough, at the moment of receiving the Body and Blood of Christ on Christmas night, to believe and say with simplicity, "Jesus, I receive you as your mother Mary received you; I love you with the love with which the heavenly Father loves you, that is, with the Holy Spirit."[78]

CHAPTER 4

Sitio, I Thirst

1. A Creative Word

In the lives of many saints, we notice that they recognized the essence of their calling and a summary of their charism in a word from God. We only need to think of the role played in the vocation of St. Anthony the Abbot by the word from the Gospel, "Go, sell what you possess and give to the poor . . . and come, follow me" (Matthew 19:21)[79] We can think of the role that the verse "Let the little children come to me" (Matthew 19:14) played in the lives of saintly educators or of the role that the verse "Mary has chosen the good portion" (Luke 10:42) played for many contemplatives.

In addition, many religious orders have a motto in their crest that encapsulates the spirituality of the founder and of his or her family. For us Franciscans, it is the motto *Deus meus et Omnia* ("My God and my all"). For the Jesuits it is *ad maiorem Dei gloriam* ("For the greater glory of God"); for the Carmelites, the word of Elijah: *Zelo zelatus sum pro Domino Deo exercituum* ("With zeal have I been zealous for the Lord God of Hosts").

It is not difficult to recognize what this key word is in the life of Mother Teresa of Calcutta: the cry of Christ on the cross, *Sitio*, "I thirst." It is written next to the crucifix on the altar of every chapel of the Missionaries of Charity. It is the saying that contains Mother Teresa's "secret." It reminds me of St. Francis' extraordinary devotion to the sign of the Tau that he drew on the walls of the monasteries, on the doors of the cells, on people's foreheads, and with which he signed the few things he wrote by his own hand.

Sitio is a word Mother Teresa received at the very moment of her second calling, but it was only toward the end of her life, overcoming no small resistance, that she decided to explain it to her daughters. The Letter of John Paul II for Lent in 1993 on the "*Sitio*" of Christ was the impetus for her decision. In the letter written at Varanasi during that same Lent, "in my own hand" and coming "from Mother's heart," she says,

> The time has come for me to speak openly of the gift God gave Sept. 10—to explain as fully as I can what means for me the thirst of Jesus. For me Jesus's thirst is something so intimate—so I have felt shy until now to speak to you of Sept. 10—I wanted to do as Our Lady who "kept all these things in her heart."
>
> That is why Mother hasn't spoken so much of I Thirst, especially outside.... For me it is so clear—everything in MC [Missionaries of Charity] exists only to satiate Jesus. His words on the wall of every MC chapel, they are not from the past only, but alive here and now, spoken to you.... Mother will try to help you understand—but Jesus himself must be the one to say to you "I Thirst."[80]

One senses that what Mother Teresa says here is just the tip of the iceberg. What she succeeds in communicating (or hopes to) is a very small part of the resonance this word from Christ had in her life. From the beginning it was a genuine mystical experience. Mother Teresa actually "heard" the dying Christ say this word in her soul. It was like an invisible "stigmata" engraved on her heart forever—a creative word. She goes on to say in that same letter, "Why does Jesus say 'I Thirst'? What does it mean? Something so hard to explain in words—if you remember anything from Mother's letter, remember this—'I thirst' is something much deeper than Jesus just saying 'I love you.'"

2. Jesus Asks in Order to Give

Typically the saints do not arrive at the truth of Scripture by exegetical paths or intellectual reflection; instead the truth comes to them with an immediacy and a power that no exegesis could ever produce. But after that, they want to know all they can about what exegesis and scholars have discovered about that saying, and they never tire of hearing about it. Let us see, then, what exegesis says about this word from Christ on the cross, and let us call to mind first of all the following passage:

> After this Jesus, knowing that all was now finished, said (to fulfil the Scripture), "*I thirst*." A bowl full of vinegar stood there; so they put a sponge full of the *vinegar* on hyssop and held it to his mouth. When Jesus had received the vinegar, he said, "It is finished"; and he bowed his head and gave up his spirit. (John 19:28-30, emphasis added)

The first meaning of this word concerns Christ's physical thirst. It does not take much effort to understand that when Christ's body, in its condition of having been scourged and bloodied, would have experienced a burning thirst. The Gospel writer sees at this moment the fulfillment of the messianic psalm (the "Scripture") that says, "My throat is parched. . . . and for my thirst they gave me vinegar to drink" (Psalm 69:3, 21).

But for John, the cry of the dying Jesus certainly also has a symbolic significance, just as every other word and gesture of Christ does at the moment of his death. One other time in his life Jesus asked for something to drink. He said to the Samaritan woman, "Give me a drink," and in response to her confused protestation he said, "If you knew the gift of God, and who it is that is saying to you, 'Give me a drink,' you would have asked him and he would have given you living water" (John 4:7, 10).

The living water Jesus promises is eternal life—concretely, the Holy Spirit. Soon after this episode at the well he will say, "'If any one thirst, let him come to me and drink. He who believes in me, as the scripture has said, "Out of his heart shall flow rivers of living water."' Now this he said about the Spirit, which those who believed in him were to receive" (John 7:37-39). It is no coincidence that after reporting the word of Christ, "I thirst," John immediately adds, "and he bowed his head and gave up his spirit" (John 19:30). On the symbolic and mystical level, this in fact means that he poured out his Spirit, the Holy Spirit, as seemingly indicated by the water and the blood pouring out of his side (see 1 John 5:8: "There are three witnesses, the Spirit, the water, and the blood.").

We understand from this that Jesus is asking in order to give; he is thirsty for us to thirst for him because only this allows him to give us living water, eternal life. He thirsts for our love and, even more, for our very being.

In response to Jesus' cry, the soldiers gave him vinegar. In the light of Psalm 69:21 ("for my thirst they gave me vinegar to drink"), this was the ultimate mockery, adding suffering to suffering, and not an attempt to alleviate his thirst or pain. This too is full of symbolic significance. It mirrors what happens in reality: humanity responds to Christ's thirst with ingratitude and insults, or with coldness and forgetfulness. In Isaiah we read a word that ancient Christian writers saw fulfilled in the death of Christ on the cross: "I spread out my hands all the day to a rebellious people" (65:2).[81]

Christ's words to St. Margaret Mary Alacoque that were crucial to the development of the devotion to the Sacred Heart of Jesus are now famous: "Behold this Heart which has so loved men that it has spared nothing. . . . In return, I receive from the greater part only ingratitude, by their irreverence and sacrilege, and by the coldness and contempt they have for Me."[82] On the day of grace and revelation, September 10, 1946, Mother Teresa must have experienced what Francis of Assisi and other saints experienced before her that prompted them to cry out, "Love is not loved! Love is not loved!"

This is the relevance of the word *Sitio*. Like all the words of the dying Christ, it runs through the centuries like a torch that is always burning. Everyone, as Mother Teresa said, should feel that this word is personally addressed to him or her, here and now. It compels you to ask yourself, "What will I give in response to Christ? The new wine of undivided love or the vinegar of compromise, lukewarmness, and withdrawal into myself?" It is not enough to do many things for Christ; he repeats to each of us what the apostle said to the Corinthians: "I seek not what is yours but you" (2 Corinthians 12:14).

3. A Message from the Pope

When Mother Teresa wrote her letter from Varanasi in 1993, it was in light of the Lenten message by the pope for that year, which had *Sitio* as its theme.[83] But what could have struck her in that message, whose theme was not so much Christ's thirst on the cross as the thirst of millions of people today afflicted by the lack of drinkable water due to the desertification of entire areas of the planet?

Mother Teresa found in that message the same indissoluble link between Jesus' *Sitio* and service to the poor which people have called "the two pillars" of her work:

> "I Thirst" and "You did it to me"—Remember always to connect the two, the means with the Aim. What God has joined together let no one split apart. Do not underestimate our practical means—the work for the poor; no matter how small or humble—that make our life something beautiful for God. They are the most precious gifts of God to our Society—Jesus's hidden presence so near, so able to touch. Without the work for the poor the Aim dies—Jesus's thirst is only words with no meaning, no answer. . . . Our charism is to satiate the thirst of Jesus for love and souls—by working at the salvation and sanctification of the poorest of the poor. [84]

The nexus Mother Teresa sees between the two things is not just subjective; it does not exist just in her heart. It is objective since it is founded on the doctrine of the mystical body. Blaise Pascal wrote, "Jesus will be in agony until the end of the world."[85] Where and how is he in agony if not in the members of his mystical body and especially in the poor and suffering? The cry "I thirst" rises up from the suffering members of the body of Christ, just as in a physical body thirst is the result of billions of cells that are urgently demanding water to survive.

As a primary need of every living organism, thirst represents all the most elementary needs of a human being: the need for water, food, but also for attention, love, a smile. A person can go without eating for days and weeks but cannot go without drinking. Those who go on hunger strikes know this well. Mother Teresa perceived in the cry of the poor an echo of Christ's cry, "I thirst!" Christ's words, "I was thirsty and you gave me to drink" (Matthew 25:35), was for her something much more real and straighforward than it is for the ordinary believer. "I" was thirsty.

4. After the Death of the Founder

Mother Teresa left the word *Sitio* as a legacy to her daughters, just as Francis of Assisi left "Lady Poverty" as a legacy to his brothers. I believe that for her this word was the reminder of a very powerful, personal, mystical experience. This does not mean that all her daughters should or can experience it in the same way Mother Teresa did. God does not press down on and flatten out his creatures; he prefers diversity and does not like "homogenization." Within her religious family as well, there is room for different sensitivities, diverse spiritual gifts, and different experiences. What Mother Teresa primarily recommended to her religious family was not that word itself but its implication: a total response to the love of Christ expressed in service to the poor.

At the death of its founder, every religious family finds itself at a crossroads. The Franciscan order I belong to experienced this in a dramatic way a few centuries ago. The crossroad consists in this: the family he or she founded can concentrate on the person of the founder, especially if he or she is canonized by the Church; they can nourish themselves on the founder's words and discuss his or her genuine spirit and charism (and often be divided over that!). Or, resisting this temptation, they can remain tenaciously focused on Christ, on "his" Spirit, on "his" words, as the founder taught them to do when he or she was alive.

When, in the formation of young people and novices through spiritual exercises and all the rest of religious life, more time is spent on speaking of the order's charism, rules, constitutions, and spirituality than on Christ the Lord and on his Holy Spirit, the center of gravity gradually shifts from God to human beings and from grace to law. St. John says the law was given through Moses but grace comes through Jesus Christ (see John 1:17). When applied to us today in the Church, this means human beings can make laws, and founders can draw up the rules for communal life and leave behind examples of holiness, but only Jesus Christ, by his Spirit, can give people the strength to live them out. I believe what Mother Teresa is saying, from heaven, to her sons and daughters, is what Francis of Assisi said to his brothers before dying: "I have done what was mine to do; may Christ teach you what you are to do."[86]

5. Mother Teresa and Mary of Bethany

Let us conclude with a modern poem about Mother Teresa that summarizes in its images what I have tried to say about the indissoluble unity for her between Christ's *Sitio* and service to the poor:

Over this dead loss to society
        you pour your precious ointment,
        wash the feet
        that will not walk tomorrow.
Mother Teresa, Mary Magdalene,
        your love is dangerous, your levity
        would contradict
        our local gravity.
But if love cannot do it, then I see
        no future for this dying man or me.
So blow the world to glory,
        crack the clock. Let love be dangerous.[87]

In the Redemptoris Mater Chapel at the Vatican, the artist Fr. Marko Rupnik has depicted a long table in his mosaics. At one end of it is Mary of Bethany who, bent over in an arc, anoints Christ's feet with perfume from a jar of precious ointment broken on one side. At the other end of the table is Jesus, in the same position as Mary, who is washing Peter's feet at the Last Supper. If I were an artist, I would depict Mother Teresa in the attitude of Mary of Bethany: on her knees, bent over to wash the feet of a poor person who, as she lifts her gaze, is revealed to be Christ sitting at the table again.

In the past, people would confuse Mary Magdalene and Mary of Bethany, the sinful woman with the contemplative evangelical, the sister of Lazarus. Today we distinguish them, and Mother Teresa should be placed alongside not the first Mary but the second one, the Mary who anoints Christ's body for his burial (see John 12:7). Mary broke the jar of precious ointment, and Mother Teresa has "cracked the clock," as the poem says. She forgot about time, which is the most precious possession we have, and she has lavished it unsparingly on the Eucharist and on the poor.

Jesus rose up to heaven but his feet remained on earth, because the feet of Christ are the poor, the poor whom Jesus said on that occasion we would always have with us (see John 12:1-8). The Eucharist, Mother Teresa reminds us, allows everyone to renew the synthesis between the response to Christ's *Sitio* and one's availability to serve the poor, between communion with his real Body and communion with his mystical body.

Mother Teresa's many prayers could be summed up in the following:

> We satiate the thirst of Jesus by adoring him in the Sacrament of the Eucharist, in our personal encounter with him, face to face. Renew your zeal to quench his thirst under the species of bread and in the sorrowful semblance of the poorest of the poor.

CHAPTER 5

The Task of Redeeming Beauty[88]

I came to Calcutta to show how the gospel is lived out and incarnated in this place in the works of Mother Teresa's daughters, the Missionary Sisters of Charity. Let us begin with a passage from the Gospel for the Second Sunday in Lent, which is the episode of the Transfiguration.

> From the Gospel according to Mark: After six days Jesus took with him Peter and James and John, and led them up a high mountain apart by themselves; and he was transfigured before them, and his garments became glistening, intensely white, as no fuller on earth could bleach them. And there appeared to them Elijah with Moses; and they were talking to Jesus. (Mark 9:2-4)

I believe this is enough of the reading for our purpose. You already know the rest of the account, and if not I urge you to read it. The true miracle of the Transfiguration was not so much that Jesus' appearance was changed; it was that the eyes of the apostles were opened, and they were able to see the divine reality, the glory of Jesus that was hidden under his ordinary human appearance.

One day the same miracle of transfiguration occurred before the eyes of Mother Teresa and made her able to see beyond appearances: she was able to see the glorious and suffering face of Christ in the disfigured faces of the dying and of abandoned babies. From that day on, Mother Teresa's adventure began; we will see her this October raised to the honors of the altar with her beatification by John Paul II, who was a great friend of hers when he was alive.

As we tour this complex, we see two classrooms for first and second grades. Before the children leave school, the sisters give them something to eat because they come from very poor families and the sisters do not want to send them home with empty stomachs. They do not do this only for the school children but also for people waiting outside the door to get rations of food, flour, and oil. Around two thousand people come every Friday to get food.

This next area, perhaps the most distressing one, is for the mentally ill and disabled. There are 240 people here. People told me about Mother Teresa's act of incredible courage to take on this work. She once visited the prisons in Calcutta. There were mentally unstable women there exposed to every kind of abuse. After having visited the female ward, Mother Teresa said to the director, "May I take care of all these women?" She took them home with her and they are here now. Of course nobody likes to witness this part of humanity, but it exists and it would be shameful for people to leave these women out on the streets. When we see this part of "disfigured" humanity, it is important to remember what St. Paul wrote to the Philippians: the Lord Jesus Christ "will change our lowly body to be like his glorious body" (Philippians 3:21). Jesus, very soon after the Transfiguration, will be "disfigured" in his passion, but he will rise again with a glorious body and live forever, and faith tells us we will be reunited with him.

We can only express gratitude to these sisters. Think of it: there are only eighteen of them and between the babies, the mentally ill, and the disabled, they have to take care of seven hundred people. They have outside collaborators and various volunteers who alternate, but the greatest weight of the care falls on their shoulders. Mother Teresa's great secret was an unbounded love for Jesus Christ and for the suffering members of his body. Today that love lives again in the work of her daughters.

In another area of the complex we see babies who are alone and abandoned or who come from very poor villages where the parents can neither look after them nor support them. At this time there are forty-five babies. The baby the sister is showing us is only one month old and is, as you can see, very small and weak. One part of the building is occupied by disabled children. They were taken in as newborns and have been growing up here. The Missionary Sisters of Charity have full responsibility for them.

The Leprosy Center here is a center for the rehabilitation of those afflicted with leprosy, for those who are healed or in the process of healing. They all practice or learn a trade. There is a workshop where prostheses are made for those who have lost a hand or a foot due to leprosy. Then there is a large workshop in which fabrics of all colors are woven. Among the various materials is also the one from which the saris for all Mother Teresa's sisters throughout the world are made. When you see a Missionary of Charity with her white sari bordered in blue, you know it came from the looms you see here.

**

Dear friends, we could say that today I brought you to the Garden of Olives instead of Tabor. I do not, however, want to leave us all with the impression of having merely visited a sample collection of poverty and human suffering. Yes, there is that, but there is also another message that this place helps us to discover in the passage about the Transfiguration, and I want to dedicate the final reflection on the Gospel passage to that.

I am struck by the title of the book that first made Mother Teresa known outside of the ecclesiastical world: *Something Beautiful for God: The Classic Account of Mother Teresa's Journey into Compassion.*[89] It chronicles the discovery that the English journalist Malcolm Muggeridge made of Mother Teresa and the religious order she founded at the end of the 1960s, when the world was not yet speaking about this extraordinary person, a symbol of Christian charity. Beauty! That seems to be the exact antithesis of what we observe here at first glance. Instead, it is the truth.

The Transfiguration is a mystery of beauty. On Tabor the disciples exclaimed, "Lord, it is well that we are here" (Mark 9:5) [the Greek word for "well," καλόν, also means "beautiful"]. The icon of the Transfiguration is the first one that every iconographer learns to paint, since it discloses the secret of "Tabor" light. The words Dostoevsky puts in the mouth of one of his favorite characters are well known: "The world will be saved by beauty." But following that affirmation, the same character immediately asks, "But what beauty will save the world?"[90] It is clear to him as well that not every beauty will save the world; there is a beauty that can save the world and a beauty that can ruin the world.

St. Paul has written, "The creation was subjected to futility, not of its own will but by the will of him who subjected it in hope; because the creation itself will be set free from its bondage to decay and obtain the glorious liberty of the children of God" (Romans 8:20-21). In place of "creation" we could substitute the word "beauty" in this text without altering the meaning of that affirmation in any way. "Beauty was subjected to futility and waits to be set free." Beauty itself, to save the world, needs to be saved. The redemption of Christ does in fact extend to beauty. Jesus has redeemed beauty, depriving himself of it out of love. St. Augustine writes about Christ,

> Because he took flesh, he took, as it were, your hideousness, that is, your mortality, that he might adapt himself to you and correspond to you and arouse you to loving beauty within. . . . "He did not have attractiveness or comeliness" [see Is 53:2], in order that he might give you attractiveness and comeliness.[91]

The model and source of redeemed beauty is that which shines in the face of Christ (see 2 Corinthians 4:6). What differentiates this redeemed beauty from every other kind of beauty, even physical beauty? It is that this beauty comes from within—that the body is the medium of its expression, not its origin. The human body becomes the "sacrament" of beauty—that is, its sign, its instrument, its manifestation, its transparency, not its ultimate source. It is not like an opaque screen on which light is cast but like a glass that lets light through. Sometimes we are aware of it when we see some of the faces of contemplatives that closely recall this mystery. But it is above all on the faces of babies (including those we have just visited) that we can grasp this beauty that emanates from the innocence and transparency of the heart.

How can we actively participate in this task of redeeming beauty? Christ, in his paschal mystery, has redeemed beauty through its opposite—that is, allowing himself be stripped of any beauty. He proclaimed there is something superior to the very *love of beauty*, and it is the *beauty of love!* It is the beauty that shines in the wrinkled face of Mother Teresa and that now (let's hope they don't hear me!) shines on the faces of her daughters.

What does all this mean for us? Does it mean that we need to renounce seeking and enjoying the created beauty in this world, especially the beauty of the human body, in expectation of the transfiguration of our bodies in the final resurrection? No, created beauty is made to embellish this life, not the future life that will have its own beauty. We can therefore enjoy created beauty if we accept with it the cross that redeems it. And the cross of beauty is not some kind of strange suffering; it is love, along with what love requires of faithfulness, of respect for the other, of obedience to God and the true meaning of things, and thus of sacrifice and renunciation.

Going from one level of beauty to a higher level—from external beauty to interior beauty and from that to the transcendent beauty of grace—does not happen in a spontaneous and painless way. It requires a spiritual discipline, and in particular in the case of beauty, a spiritual discipline of the eyes. Ludwig Feuerbach said, "Man is what he eats," but in the current culture dominated by images, perhaps it is better to say, "Man is what he looks at." More important, therefore, than shutting our eyes to false beauty is opening them to true beauty: contemplating Christ crucified and risen.

Finally, another way, but a very important one, of participating in the paschal mystery of the redemption of beauty, is to bend down toward those who, like Christ in his passion, had "no beauty that we should desire him" (Isaiah 53:2)—his poor, the tormented, the destitute today. Mother Teresa, with infinite tenderness, embracing a sick baby or an abandoned person who is dying, is part of this redeemed beauty that also redeems. It will not be, I repeat, the *love of beauty* that will save the world but *the beauty of love.*

CHAPTER 6

We Have Seen and Yet Have Believed[92]

The Gospel for tomorrow, the Sunday *in albis* ("in white"), recounts the very famous story of Thomas. Thomas is very important for India because, according to tradition, he was the apostle who brought Christianity to this country.

But let us leave aside poor St. Thomas for the moment whose initial unbelief—I don't know why—is emphasized more readily than his final act of faith. We will deal with him later. Instead I want to dedicate the first part of our time to the first reading from the Mass for the Sunday *in albis* that will now be read by Elena, who works here as a volunteer.

From the Acts of the Apostles:

> Now the company of those who believed were of one heart and soul, and no one said that any of the things which he possessed was his own, but they had everything in common. And with great power the apostles gave their testimony to the resurrection of the Lord Jesus, and great grace was upon them all. There was not a needy person among them, for as many as were possessors of lands or houses sold them, and brought the proceeds of what was sold and laid it at the apostles' feet; and distribution was made to each as any had need. (Acts 4:32-35)

I said before that I came to India to comment on the Gospel and the readings, not so much on their words as on the events in them, and that is what I want to do again this time.

This passage is speaking about the first Christian community, in which no one had any need because people had everything in common, and goods were distributed among them according to their need. Mother Teresa's sisters have done me the honor of participating for two days in the distribution of food to the many people who come here. With an apron over my habit, I too have distributed bowls of rice to the people. Let us hear from one of the sisters about the activity that takes place in this center.

"We visit families, and for those who have no clothes, medicine, or food, we give them a card so that they can come here every day to get food and medicine."

"How many people come every day?"

"Between five and six hundred."

"Where do you get all these provisions?"

"Everything depends on the donations we receive from people."

"But I see that you don't distribute only food."

"No, there is also a dispensary for treatment and medicine. When someone is hospitalized, we bring the medicine to them. The sister who is also a doctor visits the sick here. She is visiting with a young girl who has lost a baby. She is prescribing medicine that will be distributed later out here."

A human being, dear friends, needs not only food and medicine but also to be welcomed and loved. Mother Teresa said that people are hungry not just for food but also to be listened to and loved. Here we see the distribution of love. These are abandoned babies—orphans or babies from broken families—that the Sisters of Charity welcome and prepare for adoption. In the office for that, a sister is preparing documents with a photo of the baby. There are no computers here; resources and equipment are scanty, but great things are done here with meager means.

I call the room right next to this one "the room of great excitement" because it is the room in which parents meet the baby for the first time who will then be their son or daughter permanently. We are fortunate to have an Italian couple with us here to welcome the baby that is meant for them.

"My name is Margherita."

"And I am Guido, her husband. The baby's name is Aron. He is two and half years old."

"Are you feeling emotional?"

"Yes, very much so!"

"Is it a bit like giving birth to a baby?"

"Maybe even more so!"

"May God's blessing be on your whole lives! Jesus said, 'Whoever receives one such child in my name receives me,' so you are bringing home nothing less than Jesus! A small 'baby Jesus.'"

In 2000 I participated in a conference at the Vatican in the Paul VI Audience Hall for Italian and foreign families who had adopted a little boy or girl from Mother Teresa's sisters. On that occasion I was asked to give a teaching on the spiritual significance of adoption.

Dear friends, we cannot turn a blind eye to all this and not ask the question that I know is in the minds of those of you who are listening. Why bring babies into this world who will end up abandoned on the street as we see here? Here they are welcomed and treated, but that is a drop in the bucket compared to all the babies in India and in the world. Unfortunately, if we do not find a way to instill in people a sense of responsible fatherhood and motherhood, all these efforts will be inadequate. It is not just a question of distributing food (and there is enough of it on earth) but of also creating the conditions for improving the quality of life, hygiene, education. . . . The bishops here have insisted, and rightly so, on education and training. Many of these young girls get married at the age of twelve or thirteen, so we can easily imagine the problems that derive from that.

One thing I want to point out to you is that Mother Teresa did not wait for things to change structurally before acting personally. Mother Teresa put into practice the popular saying today, "Think globally, act locally." She was not unaware of the vastness and the global nature of the phenomenon of poverty, but she took action where the Lord had placed her. She took responsibility and taught us that we need to take responsibility as well. Someone once pointed out at a meeting that all her work was only a drop in the ocean compared to the needs in the world. She replied that it was true, but "the ocean is made up of drops!"[93]

Mother Teresa, without realizing it, took the anecdote by the Indian author Anthony de Mello literally. A man saw a baby girl shivering from the cold, hurt and suffering. He had a surge of rebellion and shouted to God, "God, why don't you do something for this baby?" And he heard a response within himself: "Of course I have done something for her: I created you!" Mother Teresa took this literally. She taught us that each of us can do something for someone else.

At the Dance School for Young Girls at Shishu Bhavan

Mother Teresa, I said the last time, wanted to do something beautiful for God. She succeeded! And this is something beautiful not only for God but also for everybody. Tell me if it is not a beautiful thing to see these young seven-year-old girls picked up from the streets now performing some traditional Indian dances! What grace and simplicity! A French poet, Charles Péguy, wrote a poem on the three theological virtues. In it he represents Hope as a young girl in the middle pulling her two big sisters, Faith and Charity, behind her. I propose that you name this young girl "Child Hope" and that we make her a symbol of the future of India and of the world.

**

And now, as always, let us spend time on a more direct reflection on the Gospel. Tomorrow, as I said, is the Sunday *in albis*, "in white." It is called this because in ancient times neophytes returned to church on this day in the white garments of their Baptism. The Gospel tells us of two apparitions of Christ that took place in the Cenacle eight days apart. In the first episode, Easter night, the apostle Thomas was not present. When the others told him what happened, he made his famous declaration, "Unless I see in his hands the print of the nails, and place my finger in the mark of the nails, and place my hand in his side, I will not believe" (John 20:25). Now let us hear what follows in that Gospel:

Eight days later, his disciples were again in the house, and Thomas was with them. The doors were shut, but Jesus came and stood among them, and said, "Peace be with you." Then he said to Thomas, "Put your finger here, and see my hands; and put out your hand, and place it in my side; do not be faithless, but believing." Thomas answered him, "My Lord and my God!" Jesus said to him, "You have believed because you have seen me. Blessed are those who have not seen and yet believe." (John 20:26-29)

In emphasizing the story of Thomas, the Gospel meets modern readers halfway—people in the technological era who only believe what they can verify. It presents them a credible model, someone who resembles them enough to be taken into consideration: Thomas, the doubter, the practical man, the one who declares it will not be easy to persuade him to surrender and believe! We can call Thomas our contemporary among the apostles.

What saved Thomas was his suffering over his unbelief. The severity of the stipulations he imposed in order to believe (putting his hand in Jesus' side, his finger in the wounds) comes from his great distress. He is the one among the apostles who had the most regrets about not having died with Jesus as he had earlier solemnly declared he would do (see John 11:16). But suffering for not loving someone is already a sign of love. Suffering for not being able to believe is a form of faith, incomplete but sincere!

A famous journalist once said in an interview,

I have always sought God and have not found him. I have always looked for him because I believe that faith can give a person extraordinary strength. But I don't feel personally responsible or guilty because I lack this strength. And if I found God I would ask him, "Why didn't you give me faith?"

To him and to all those who find themselves in this same situation, I recall what believers like St. Augustine and Blaise Pascal felt they heard from God: "You would not seek me if you had not found me."[94] Desiring without believing can be a purer faith than believing without desiring and taking everything for granted.

Thomas had stated an absurd requirement, a far-fetched challenge, formulated in the passionate fervor of his resistance: "If I do not see . . . if I do not place my finger there . . . ." Jesus nonetheless accepts his requirement (John 20:25). He lets himself be won over by Thomas. Only for Thomas does Jesus change his instructions and his approach. For example, he had said the opposite to Magdalene: "Do not touch me!" (see John 20:17). Jesus loved Thomas. He knew that Thomas was so reluctant only because he had felt so distressed, so he sided with him; he spoke to his heart, and Thomas was overwhelmed.

When Thomas saw Jesus standing before him, he immediately understood that he had always known that Jesus was risen. He had lived long enough with Jesus to know that he should have expected something like this, that with Jesus there were always wonderful, incredible things like this happening! He should have believed the others. In refusing to believe, he had only inflicted punishment on himself, guarding himself against an expectation that was too acute—like someone saying to himself, "That's too good to be true!" He was conflicted by both the desire to believe and the fear of believing.

Now he no longer desires to touch; he would have given anything to avoid putting his finger and his hand in the wounds and not to hear that veiled reproof, "You have believed because you have seen me. Blessed are those who have not seen and yet believe" (John 20:29). And when he does touch Jesus, he does it with docility, in repentance. Modern artists have depicted "the first Thomas," the one who still wants to see and touch; ancient painters, who were more spiritual, especially in Eastern icons, represent him bent in adoration, like someone who is intending to fall to the ground before Jesus.

To have such deep intimacy with Christ, Thomas was transported to a height that none of the others had reached up to that point—higher even than John, who was the only one allowed to lay his head on Jesus' chest, but that was still external to Jesus. Overwhelmed, astounded, Thomas falls to his knees and exclaims, "My Lord and my God!" (John 20:28). None of the other apostles had yet been impelled to say to Jesus, "My God!" Jesus loved Thomas so much that he healed him with great tenderness by exchanging his guilt and humiliation for a wonderful memory. This is how Christ remits sins. He knows how to make all human faults into "happy faults" (as the *Exultet* in the Easter liturgy says), faults that we no longer remember except for the wonderful tenderness they occasioned!

St. Gregory the Great says that Thomas, because of his unbelief, is more useful for us than all the other apostles who believed instantly. Thomas forced Jesus, so to speak, to give us a "tangible" proof of the truth of his resurrection. Faith in the resurrection benefited from his doubts. This is also true, at least in part, when applied to the numerous "Thomases" today who are nonbelievers. The Second Vatican Council declared that the Church acknowledges having learned much from those who have fought against it. Meeting with nonbelievers helps us purify our faith from crude representations. Very often what nonbelievers reject is not the true God, the living God of the Bible, but a poor imitation—a distorted image of God that believers themselves have helped to create. In rejecting that God, nonbelievers occasionally force us, in a healthy way, to return to seeking the true and living God, who is beyond all of our representations and explanations, and to avoid petrifying or trivializing God.

We cannot, however, conclude our reflection on today's Gospel on this optimistic note. There is at least one wish we have: that St. Thomas would find many imitators today, not just in the first part of his story when he declares he does not believe, but also in the second part and above all in the final part in his magnificent act of faith. Thomas is to be imitated by nonbelievers for another reason. He did not close the door; he did not remain fixed in his position, having settled the issue once and for all. This is clearly the case since eight days later we find him with the other apostles in the Cenacle again. If he had not wanted to believe, or change his mind, he would not have been there. He wanted to see and touch, so he was seeking. And at the end, after he saw and touched with his hand, he exclaimed to Jesus, not as a loser but as a winner, "My Lord and my God!" Thomas returned to faith again by touching Jesus' wounds. Many nonbelievers, who have come to this place to help Mother Teresa's daughters, have found faith by touching the wounds of the body of Christ—the poor.

As for us believers, the story of Thomas exhorts us to appreciate the privilege we have. We can still believe before forcing God's hand to make himself seen and touched through signs and miracles. We can believe "before seeing." In fact we can be among "those who have seen and yet have believed,"[95] as the paradox from G. K. Chesterton says. We can be among those who see all the human misery there has been—and that still is—in the Church and nevertheless have not lost faith in Christ or in the Church.

CHAPTER 7

Whoever Receives One Such Child in My Name Receives Me[96]

Emotion throughout the world over the death of Mother Teresa of Calcutta has still not subsided, and we are here to celebrate one of the most beautiful fruits of her work: the care of orphan or abandoned children. In October 1984 I had the privilege of embracing Mother Teresa in this very hall during the first World Retreat for Priests. I am sure that, by her spirit, she is present today as well in this room and is blessing the families who have adopted a child and those who have worked to make this possible.

The small contribution I can offer to the couples who have adopted a boy or a girl—and to the Missionaries of Charity who acted as intermediaries—is a reflection on the spiritual and human significance of adoption. St. Paul used the image of adoption to illustrate our relationship with God: "When the time had fully come, God sent forth his Son . . . so that we might receive adoption as sons" (Galatians 4:4-5). He explains what the basis for this adoption is. It is based on the fact that the natural Son of God, Jesus Christ, in becoming man, took us on as brothers and sisters. He has given us his Spirit and has united us to himself as members to the head, making us one single family: "Because you are sons, God has sent the Spirit of his Son into our hearts, crying, 'Abba! Father!' So through

God you are no longer a slave but a son, and if a son then an heir" (Galatians 4:6-7).

This took place, in a certain sense, in the reverse order of human adoptions. In human adoptions, it is the father and mother who adopt, and if they have natural children, they try to help them welcome the little brother or sister that is being added to the family. Here, on the contrary, it is the older brother, Jesus, who adopts us and presents us to the Father in one Spirit (see Ephesians 2:16). We first became brothers and sisters and then sons and daughters, even if the two things happened simultaneously at Baptism. We became "sons and daughters in the Son."

In the deepest sense we are all adopted sons and daughters ourselves, even those of you who are here as adoptive fathers and mothers; you have been adopted before becoming adopters. Precisely because of this analogy, adoptive fathers and mothers have something important to learn from God and to teach us about God.

Adoption can at times be an experience of great suffering. Adopted children often carry with them the traumas of the situation they came from that can manifest as rebellion, violence, and an usual form of apparent rejection and ingratitude. But just as there is a grace for the state of matrimony, so too there must be a grace for the state of being adoptive parents, because they often demonstrate an understanding and a patience that is almost superhuman. They rise to a level of love that, on earth, is one that reminds us the most of God's love: a gratuitous love that "bears all things, believes all things, hopes all things, endures all things" (1 Corinthians 13:7).

In observing some adoptive parents, I have understood some things about God the Father that cannot be learned from any theological book. Seeing the generosity and perseverance of their love and their capacity for finding an excuse, or at least a mitigating circumstance, for everything, I said to myself, this is precisely what the heavenly Father does with us! We often drag his name into the dust; we even come to the point of blaming him for bringing us into the world. But he continues, with immense patience and magnanimity, to call us sons and daughters. He never disowns us even when we deny him and bring shame to him. "If we are faithless, he remains faithful—for he cannot deny himself" (2 Timothy 2:13).

But adoption, thanks be to God, is most often a source of very great, sheer joy. I knew a couple who had nine children of their own and who adopted another five—all from other continents except the first child. For years they had to struggle to save that first adopted child from a serious illness. That young girl now, happily married and the mother of two children herself, has asked her adoptive parents to help her adopt a baby. The father told me, "That has been the best reward we could ever have wished for." He was right. In adopting children, he and his wife not only resolved a human predicament but also set in motion a chain of solidarity that is ongoing.

Often the little adopted boy or girl develops a kind of very special love for those who have taken them out of solitude, poverty, and marginalization. It is a love of emotional gratitude and admiration that we do not encounter in any other human situation. Perhaps the children do not think of it and do not succeed in expressing it in words, but it is there in the depth of their hearts, and one day perhaps they will make their parents melt into tears.

I would also like, in fact, to address a brief word in this regard to the children present, at least to those who are able to hear my words or who in some way will become aware of them: "Don't wait too long to do it!" In my television ministry, I receive many letters, but there is one I have never forgotten. It was from a boy who had recently lost his father and was inconsolable. Only then did he realize what his father meant to him; he was not at peace for not having told him before and felt the need to go tell him now, weeping at his tomb.

That gave me the idea of often recommending to young people, when I have the chance to talk to them, that they use the occasion of an anniversary or a family celebration to thank their dad and mom. Not an ordinary thank you for this or that small gift or permission to do something. Tell them, "Thank you for the life you have given me; thank you for being there; thank you for being my dad, and thank you for being my mom." Do not wait until you have to say it to them weeping at their grave. If you are embarrassed to say it out loud, then write it down, for example, in a little note; in my time good little boys and girls put notes under the plates of their parents on Christmas Eve. But while we teach children to say thank you, let us not forget to say it to God, because as we have seen, we are all his adoptive children.

* *

Now for the most consoling word for adoptive fathers and mothers. It is Jesus who is speaking to you, not I.

And he took a child, and put him in the midst of them; and taking him in his arms, he said to them, "Whoever receives one such child in my name receives me; and whoever receives me, receives not me but him who sent me." (Mark 9:36-37)

Jesus wanted to remain present in the world in many ways: in his word, in the Eucharist, in his visible representatives ("he who hears you hears me"[97]), in the poor ("You did it to me"[98]). Another one of these ways—incredible, but true—is in the child.

If we ask why Jesus had a predilection for children, the answer is not difficult. Little children have no influence; they cannot advance anyone's career or increase anyone's prestige. They do nothing for you; they need you to do things for them. It is easy to cultivate a friendship with someone who can give you something or be useful to you. "What credit is it to you," asks Jesus, "when you greet those who greet you or invite to dinner those who can invite you in return? Everyone already does that, including the Gentiles" (see Luke 6:32-34).

Jesus' predilection for children has the same root as his predilection for the poor, for the unimportant, for those at the bottom because this is how his Father acts: "I thank you, Father, Lord of heaven and earth, that you have hidden these things from the wise and understanding and revealed them to infants; yes, Father, for such was your gracious will" (Matthew 11:25-26).

Are you thinking about the honor that Jesus has given you? He is the one you have adopted; he is the one who has entered your house with the baby boy or girl that you have welcomed. "He receives me." We read about the following episode in the life of Origen, one of the greatest writers in antiquity who lived in the third century at the time of the persecution by Decius. At a certain point during a get-together after Origen's Baptism,

Leonides, his father, disappeared. They looked for him and found him on his knees before the cradle of his son who was just baptized, kissing him on the forehead. When they asked him what he was doing, he said, "I am kissing God, who inhabits the heart of my son as of today."[99] You too can come near the child you have adopted, perhaps when the child is sleeping, and kiss him or her on the forehead, saying, "I am kissing Jesus Christ, who is present with us in this little boy or girl."

The verse "Whoever receives one such child in my name receives me" (Mark 9:37) is of course addressed not just to adoptive fathers and mothers but also to couples who open themselves to welcome a new life that has come from them naturally. This is something that is now becoming almost an exception—at least in Italy. There are no more children or there are very few. Our country is full of preschools and elementary schools that are closing or are being "repurposed." We are becoming a nation of old people.

Sometimes people blame economic factors and taxes for this. These reasons comes into play too, but that is not the main reason. Otherwise births would increase gradually as we move up to the highest levels of society or as long as we go from the south to the north in Italy, but we know exactly the opposite is true.

The main reason goes deeper: it is the lack of hope! If getting married is always an act of faith, then bringing a child into the world, just like adopting, is always an act of hope. We are a nation that has lost hope and with it the vital impetus, the joy, the capacity for looking ahead to the future. We forgo the essential for the ephemeral: we give up authentic, intense joys for another trip, another comfort, an extra freedom. We are like a tree that has lost its deepest roots and is now being nourished only through its superficial roots.

When hope is reborn in a situation, everything looks different, even if nothing has in fact changed. Hope is a primordial force. It literally brings about miracles. I am the kind of person who is sensitive to cold, and I have noticed one thing: the temperature in Italy in April and November is more or less the same. But the cold weather in April makes me less afraid, and I can withstand it better than the cold weather in November. Why? It's obvious: in April spring is coming and in November winter is coming. The cold weather in April is with hope, while the cold weather in November is without hope.

* *

The best gift that Jesus can give you in this meeting, in this jubilee year and the anniversary of Mother Teresa's birth in heaven, is that of increasing or of rekindling Hope in each or you!—Hope with a capital "H", the theological virtue of Hope, the mother and support of all hopes, even human and earthly ones.

What is theological Hope? It is a new capacity, given to whoever believes. It grafts itself onto our natural capacity to look forward to the future, which is simple human hope, giving it a new incentive and new content. It imparts a "wide open" horizon that is no longer bounded by any walls or hedges—not even that of death.

Hope, together with Faith and Charity, is one of three divine shoots or seeds that the Spirit plants in the life of the baptized, one of the three "resources" that Christ has created for human beings. "By his great mercy we have been born anew to a living hope through the resurrection of Jesus Christ from the dead" (1 Peter 1:3). "Born anew" means a new birth, a new youth. St. Paul defines the Christian God as "the God of hope" (Romans 15:13).

The poet Charles Péguy has written a poem on the theological virtue of Hope. At a certain point he more or less says this: Faith, Hope, and Charity are like three sisters who walk happily down the street holding hands. Two of them are older, and the one in the middle is a child. (And we understand who that child is.) Everyone who sees them thinks that the two older ones, Faith and Charity, are leading the child. Instead it is exactly the opposite: it is the child Hope who is leading the other two, because if Hope stops they all stop. We see this in life as well.

The poet goes on to say that just like the faithful who, as they exited the church, once passed holy water from hand to hand, so too Christians must pass down divine hope from father and mother to son and daughter. This meeting would remain a blessing for your whole lives if each couple were infected by the hope of the others, if it combined everyone's hope in such a way that you would go home with a new enthusiasm and new courage in your hearts, ready to spread hope around you and to motivate others to open up to life.

You have adopted a little boy or girl, so adopt another: the child Hope! Take her home this very day, holding her hand tight. She will make everything easier and better. Hope will instead be the one to lead you. The apostles said to Jesus, "Increase our faith!" (Luke 17:5); let us ask him to increase our hope!

Long live the institution of adoption! Long live Mother Teresa and her daughters who, with so much love and self-lessness, have made this possible for you. These sisters in their blue and white habits spread hope and joy throughout the world. Even the darkest places are illuminated wherever they appear. If they did not exist, isn't it true that we would need to invent them—to invent them to bring a new soul and a new spirit into the complicated, and not always transparent, world of adoption as well?

My sincerest best wishes go to all you adoptive fathers and mothers. You have discovered today that you are in good company because God is an adoptive Father, and the Blessed Mother, in a different but real way, is an adoptive mother—from the moment she also adopted you as the younger brothers and sisters of her son Jesus. May you have joy from your children and help from God and the Blessed Virgin in difficult times. May God bless all of you!

BIOGRAPHICAL TIMELINE OF MOTHER TERESA'S LIFE

1910
On August 26, Mother Teresa is born Agnes Gonxha Bojax-hiu in Skopje, Albania. She is the third and last child of Nikola Bojaxhiu and Drana Bernai. Her parents, especially her mother, were devout Catholics. Agnes' father died when she was only nine years old.

1922
At the age of twelve, Agnes experiences a desire to dedicate her life to God and become a missionary.

1928
At the age of eighteen, Agnes again feels a strong desire to be a missionary, and joins the Sisters of Our Lady of Loreto, a group of nuns who work in India. She leaves her family and goes to Dublin, Ireland, to the motherhouse of Our Lady of Loreto. After a brief stay to study English, she leaves for India.

1929
Agnes begins her novitiate at the Loreto convent in Darjeel-ing, taking on the name "Sister Teresa" out of devotion to St. Thérèse of Lisieux.

1931
After two years of novitiate, Sr. Teresa makes her simple vows. Her first assignment is to teach geography and history at St. Mary's High School, run by her community in Calcutta.

1937

On May 24, she takes her final vows. As was the custom for Loreto nuns, she took on the title of "Mother" upon making her final vows and thus became known as Mother Teresa.

1946

On September 10, on a train trip to Darjeeling, Mother Teresa experiences the "call within a call"—to dedicate herself entirely to the poorest of the poor. This day is now known as her Day of Inspiration among the Missionaries of Charity.

In October, she confides her experience to her mother superior, but encounters hostility and distrust from her community.

1948

After examining her ideas at length, Archbishops Périer of Calcutta writes to Pope Pius XII requesting "secularization" for the nun who wants to begin her new work outside the convent. The Vatican responds to Archbishop Périer's letter and grants "exclaustration" rather than the "secularization" he had requested. Mother Teresa now has permission to remain a nun while living outside the convent.

On August 16, Mother Teresa puts on a white sari instead of the religious habit of the Sisters of Our Lady of Loreto and leaves the convent to fulfill her new mission. She later said that parting from Loreto was harder than saying goodbye to her family and her country.

She spends three months taking basic medical training in first aid and nursing care at the hospital of the Medical Missionary Sisters in Patna. She then returns to Calcutta and chooses December 25 as the first day to begin her service to the poorest of the poor.

1949

On the Feast of St. Joseph, Mother Teresa's first companion, Agnes, join her.

1950

With ten companions working with her, she writes the Rule of the congregation that she is forming. Archbishop Périer examines the document and sends it to Rome. On October 7, news arrives of the Vatican's approval for the new congregation of the Missionaries of Charity.

1952

Mother Teresa founds her first major house of social services, Nirmal Hriday, the Home for the Dying Destitute.

1953

Nearly thirty Missionaries of Charity take up residence at their official motherhouse. Air conditioners, electric fans, washing machines, and other modern comforts are not allowed there.

1954

She founds Shishu Bhavan, the Home for Children.

1956

She founds Shanti Naghar, the village for those with leprosy.

1960

Mother Teresa leaves India for the first time and goes to America for a conference. On her return she stops in Rome, and, through the assistance of Cardinal Gregorio Agagianian, her request for the Missionaries of Charity to become a congregation of pontifical right is presented to Pope John XXIII.

1962

Mother Teresa's work continues to grow and elicits great admiration. The president of India awards her the Padma Shri prize, and the president of the Philippines awards her the Magsaysay Prize.

1963

On March 25, the archbishop of Calcutta approves the male branch of Mother Teresa's work, the Missionaries of Charity Brothers.

1964

Pope Paul VI meets with Mother Teresa during his trip to Bombay. To express his esteem and admiration, he donates to her the luxury car he had used for his meetings throughout India.

1965

On February 1, Pope Paul VI grants the pontifical right to Mother Teresa's congregation.

1965

On July 26, Mother Teresa goes to Cocorote, Venezuela, and founds her first house outside of India.

1967

On December 8, she opens a house in Colombo, Sri Lanka.

1968

On August 22, she opens her first center in Rome.

1968

On September 8, she opens a house in Tabora, Tanzania.

1969

On March 26, Pope Paul VI approves the International Association of the Co-Workers of Mother Teresa.

On September 13, Mother Teresa opens a center for Aborigines in Bourke, Australia.

1970

On July 16, she opens a house in Amman, Jordan.

On December 8, she opens a novitiate house for the Missionaries of Charity in London.

1971

On January 6, she receives the Pope John XXIII Peace Prize in Rome from Pope Paul VI.

In September, she receives the Good Samaritan Award in Boston, Massachusetts.

In October, she opens a house in Belfast, Northern Ireland, and another in the Bronx, New York.

1972

On September 15, Mother Teresa receives the Jawaharlal Nehru Prize for International Understanding from the government of India.

1973

On April 25, Prince Philip of England confers on Mother Teresa the Templeton Prize for the Promotion of Religion.

On October 20 Mother Teresa takes part in a solidarity march in Milan, Italy, and receives the Ambrogino d'Oro, a gold medal, from the mayor.

1975

On December 29, *Time* magazine has a drawing of Mother Teresa on its cover with the inscription: "Living Saints: Messengers of Love and Hope."

1976

On January 17, Mother Teresa is on the cover of *Paris Match*, a French weekly magazine.

On August 6, she gives a speech in Philadelphia, Pennsylvania, at the 41st International Eucharistic Congress.

1979

On March 1, President Sandro Pertini of Italy presents Mother Teresa with the international Balzan Prize.

1979

On October 17, Mother Teresa receives the Nobel Peace Prize in Oslo, Norway.

1980

On January 25, she receives the highest civilian award of India, the Bharat Ratna (Jewel of India).

1981

In May, the Faculty of Medicine at the Catholic University of the Sacred Heart in Milan grants her an honorary medical degree.

1983

In August, she is hospitalized and given a pacemaker.

1988

In February, she goes to Moscow to get permission from the Communist government to open a house in the Soviet capital.

1990

In March, after repeated heart attacks, Mother Teresa tenders her resignation as superior general of her congregation. In September, however, the general chapter meeting of the congregation unanimously reelects Mother Teresa as superior and she accepts.

1991

In March, Mother Teresa returns to her native country, Albania, and takes part in the ceremony for the reopening of the cathedral in Tirana, which had been made into a theater during the Communist regime. She opens three houses for charitable works in that country.

1992

Mother Teresa meets Princess Diana, the wife of Prince Charles of England, in Calcutta. Diana is going through a difficult period in her life, and Mother Teresa invites her to dedicate herself to volunteer work. A friendship is established between the two women.

1993

Mother Teresa contracts malaria in India. When she later has another serious heart attack, she is hospitalized in the Birla Heart Research Centre in Calcutta. She is given a second pacemaker.

1996

On May 21, she is made an Honorary Citizen of Rome by Mayor Francesco Rutelli at the Campidoglio in Rome.

On August 20, Mother Teresa is hospitalized in the Woodlands Hospital in Calcutta after yet another heart attack. Doctors discover that she still tests positive for the malaria she had contracted in 1993.

1996

On November 26, speaking from a hospital in Calcutta after one more heart attack, she says, "Let me die in peace like my destitute people."

On November 29, she receives a heart operation with angioplasty in New Delhi.

1997

In March, Mother Teresa again tenders her resignation as superior general of the congregation. The community accepts it and elects Sr. Nirmala Joshi in her place.

In June, Mother Teresa and Princess Diana meet in the Bronx, New York, for their last time together.

On June 29, she meets with Pope John Paul II in Rome for the last time.

On September 1, Mother Teresa hears the news about the tragic death of Diana and expresses great sorrow and offers prayers for the princess.

On September 5, at 9:30 p.m., while she is preparing to go to bed in the General House in Calcutta, Mother Teresa has her last heart attack and dies.

On September 6, news of Mother Teresa's death is reported worldwide. The world grieves profoundly.

On September 7, before his televised recitation of the Angelus from Castel Gandolfo, Pope John Paul II commemorates Mother Teresa, calling her, among other things, "a very dear sister," and pointing to her as an "eloquent example" for believers.

On September 9, Cardinal Joseph Ratzinger, during a press conference, also speaks of Mother Teresa and says, "I believe that in Mother Teresa's case, the process of beatification can go forward in an expedited manner since her life was so transparent and luminous."

On September 13, Mother Teresa's state funeral is televised throughout the world with heads of states, royalty, and important representatives from many nations in attendance. In the afternoon her body is entombed in the General House of her congregation in Calcutta.

1998

On September a young woman in India, an animist, Monica Besra, who was stricken with a serious tumor, invokes Mother Teresa's help and is suddenly healed.

1999

On July 26, the process of beatification for Mother Teresa begins. According to canon law, this process can begin only after five years have passed since the death of that person. However, Pope John Paul II makes an exception for Mother Teresa.

2001

On July 14, Cardinal Henry S. D'Souza, the archbishop of Calcutta, announces that the diocesan process for beatification is completed.

2002

In October, the Vatican Congregation for the Causes of Saints approves Mother Teresa's life of extraordinary moral virtue and the miracle from her intercession.

On December 20, Pope John Paul II solemnly promulgates the decrees regarding Mother Teresa's life of heroic virtue and the miracle from her intercession.

2003

On October 19, Pope John Paul II celebrates the solemn ceremony of beatification of Mother Teresa in St. Peter's Square with more than 300,000 people in attendance.

2015

On December 17, the Vatican Press Office confirms that a second miracle is attributed to Mother Teresa: the healing of a Brazilian man with multiple brain tumors in 2008.

2016

On September 4, Pope Francis celebrates the canonization of Mother Teresa, now St. Teresa of Calcutta. Tens of thousands of people witness the ceremony, including 15 government delegations and 1,500 homeless people from across Italy. Skopje, Mother Teresa's hometown, announces a week-long celebration of her canonization.

Beatification of Mother Teresa of Calcutta

Homily of His Holiness John Paul II

Sunday, October 19, 2003

"*Whoever would be first among you must be slave of all*" (Mk 10:44). Jesus' words to his disciples that have just rung out in this Square show us the way to evangelical "greatness." It is the way walked by Christ himself that took him to the Cross: a journey of love and service that overturns all human logic. *To be the servant of all!*

Mother Teresa of Calcutta, Foundress of the Missionaries of Charity whom today I have the joy of adding to the Roll of the Blesseds, allowed this logic to guide her. I am personally grateful to this courageous woman whom I have always felt beside me. Mother Teresa, *an icon of the Good Samaritan*, went everywhere to serve Christ in the poorest of the poor. Not even conflict and war could stand in her way.

Every now and then she would come and tell me about her experiences in her service to the Gospel values. I remember, for example, her pro-life and anti-abortion interventions, even when she was awarded the Nobel Prize for peace (Oslo, 10

December 1979). She often used to say: "If you hear of some woman who does not want to keep her child and wants to have an abortion, try to persuade her to bring him to me. I will love that child, seeing in him the sign of God's love."

Is it not significant that her beatification is taking place on the very day on which the Church celebrates *World Mission Sunday?* With the witness of her life, Mother Teresa reminds everyone that *the evangelizing mission of the Church passes through charity*, nourished by prayer and listening to God's word. Emblematic of this missionary style is the image that shows the new Blessed clasping a child's hand in one hand while moving her Rosary beads with the other.

Contemplation and action, evangelization and human promotion: Mother Teresa proclaimed the Gospel living her life *as a total gift to the poor* but, at the same time, *steeped in prayer.*

"*Whoever wants to be great among you must be your servant*" (Mk 10:43). With particular emotion we remember today Mother Teresa, a great servant of the poor, of the Church and of the whole world. Her life is a testimony to the dignity and the privilege of humble service. She had chosen to be not just *the least* but to be *the servant of the least.* As a real mother to the poor, she bent down to those suffering various forms of poverty. Her greatness lies in her ability to give without counting the cost, to give "until it hurts." Her life was a radical living and a bold proclamation of the Gospel.

The cry of Jesus on the Cross, "*I thirst*" (Jn 19:28), expressing the depth of God's longing for man, penetrated Mother Teresa's soul and found fertile soil in her heart. *Satiating Jesus' thirst for love and for souls* in union with Mary, the Mother of Jesus, had become the sole aim of Mother Teresa's existence and the inner force that drew her out of herself and made her "run in haste" across the globe to labour for the salvation and the sanctification of the poorest of the poor.

"*As you did to one of the least of these my brethren, you did it to me*" (Mt 25:40). This Gospel passage, so crucial in understanding Mother Teresa's service to the poor, was the basis of her faith-filled conviction that *in touching the broken bodies of the poor she was touching the body of Christ.* It was to Jesus himself, hidden under the distressing disguise of the poorest of the poor, that her service was directed. Mother Teresa highlights the deepest meaning of service—an act of love done to the hungry, thirsty, strangers, naked, sick, prisoners (cf. Mt 25:34-36) is done to Jesus himself.

Recognizing him, she ministered to him with wholehearted devotion, expressing the delicacy of her spousal love. Thus, in total gift of herself to God and neighbour, Mother Teresa found her greatest fulfilment and *lived the noblest qualities of her femininity.* She wanted to be a sign of "God's love, God's presence and God's compassion," and so remind all of the value and dignity of each of God's children, "created to love and be loved." Thus was Mother Teresa "bringing souls to God and God to souls" and satiating Christ's thirst, especially for those most in need, those whose vision of God had been dimmed by suffering and pain.

"*The Son of man also came . . . to give his life as a ransom for many*" (Mk 10:45). Mother Teresa shared in the Passion of the crucified Christ in a special way during long years of "inner darkness." For her that was a test, at times an agonizing one, which she accepted as a rare "gift and privilege."

In the darkest hours she clung even more tenaciously to prayer before the Blessed Sacrament. This harsh spiritual trial led her to *identify herself more and more closely with those whom she served each day,* feeling their pain and, at times, even their rejection. She was fond of repeating that *the greatest poverty is to be unwanted,* to have no one to take care of you.

"*Lord, let your mercy be on us, as we place our trust in you.*" How often, like the Psalmist, did Mother Teresa call on her Lord in times of inner desolation: "In you, in you I hope, my God!"

Let us praise the Lord for this *diminutive woman in love with God,* a humble Gospel messenger and a tireless benefactor of humanity. In her we honour one of the most important figures of our time. Let us welcome her message and follow her example.

Virgin Mary, Queen of all the Saints, help us to be gentle and humble of heart like this fearless messenger of Love. Help us to serve every person we meet with joy and a smile. Help us to be missionaries of Christ, our peace and our hope. Amen!

Holy Mass and Canonization of Blessed Mother Teresa of Calcutta

Homily of His Holiness Pope Francis

Sunday, September 4, 2016

"Who can learn the counsel of God?" (*Wis* 9:13). This question from the Book of Wisdom that we have just heard in the first reading suggests that our life is a mystery and that we do not possess the key to understanding it. There are always two protagonists in history: God and man. Our task is to perceive the call of God and then to do his will. But in order to do his will, we must ask ourselves, "What is God's will in my life?"

We find the answer in the same passage of the Book of Wisdom: "People were taught what pleases you" (*Wis* 9:18). In order to ascertain the call of God, we must ask ourselves and understand what pleases God. On many occasions the prophets proclaimed what was pleasing to God. Their message found a wonderful synthesis in the words "I want mercy, not sacrifice" (*Hos* 6:6; *Mt* 9:13). God is pleased by every act of mercy, because in the brother or sister that we assist, we recognize the face of God which no one can see (cf. *John* 1:18). Each time we bend down to the needs of our brothers and sisters, we give Jesus something to eat and drink; we clothe, we help, and we visit the Son of God (cf. *Mt* 25:40). In a word, we touch the flesh of Christ.

We are thus called to translate into concrete acts that which we invoke in prayer and profess in faith. There is no alternative to charity: those who put themselves at the service of others, even when they don't know it, are those who love God (cf. *1 Jn* 3:16-18; *Jas* 2:14-18). The Christian life, however, is not merely extending a hand in times of need. If it is just this, it can be, certainly, a lovely expression of human solidarity which offers immediate benefits, but it is sterile because it lacks roots. The task which the Lord gives us, on the contrary, is the *vocation to charity* in which each of Christ's disciples puts his or her entire life at his service, so to grow each day in love.

We heard in the Gospel, "Large crowds were travelling with Jesus" (*Lk* 14:25). Today, this "large crowd" is seen in the great number of volunteers who have come together for the Jubilee of Mercy. You are that crowd who follows the Master and who makes visible his concrete love for each person. I repeat to you the words of the Apostle Paul: "I have indeed received much joy and comfort from your love, because the hearts of the saints have been refreshed through you" (*Philem* 1:7). How many hearts have been comforted by volunteers! How many hands they have held; how many tears they have wiped away; how much love has been poured out in hidden, humble and selfless service! This praiseworthy service gives voice to the faith—it gives voice to the faith!—and expresses the mercy of the Father, who draws near to those in need.

Following Jesus is a serious task, and, at the same time, one filled with joy; it takes a certain daring and courage to recognize the divine Master in the poorest of the poor and those who are cast aside, and to give oneself in their service. In order to do so, volunteers, who out of love of Jesus serve the poor and the needy, do not expect any thanks or recompense; rather they renounce all this because they have discovered true love. And each one of us can say: "Just as the Lord has come to meet me and has stooped down to my level in my hour of need, so too do I go to meet him, bending low before those who have lost faith or who live as though God did not exist, before young people without values or ideals, before families in crisis, before the ill and the imprisoned, before refugees and immigrants, before the weak and defenceless in body and spirit, before abandoned children, before the elderly who are on their own. Wherever someone is reaching out, asking for a helping hand in order to get up, this is where our presence—and the presence of the Church which sustains and offers hope—must be." And I do this, keeping alive the memory of those times when the Lord's hand reached out to me when I was in need.

Mother Teresa, in all aspects of her life, was a generous dispenser of divine mercy, making herself available for everyone through her welcome and defence of human life, those unborn and those abandoned and discarded. She was committed to defending life, ceaselessly proclaiming that "the unborn are the weakest, the smallest, the most vulnerable." She bowed down before those who were spent, left to die on the side of the road, seeing in them their God-given dignity; she made her voice heard before the powers of this world, so that they might recognize their guilt for the crime—the crimes!—of poverty they created. For Mother Teresa, mercy was the "salt" which gave flavour to her work, it was the "light" which shone in the darkness of the many who no longer had tears to shed for their poverty and suffering.

Her mission to the urban and existential peripheries remains for us today an eloquent witness to God's closeness to the poorest of the poor. Today, I pass on this emblematic figure of womanhood and of consecrated life to the whole world of volunteers: may she be your model of holiness! I think, perhaps, we may have some difficulty in calling her "Saint Teresa": her holiness is so near to us, so tender and so fruitful that we continue to spontaneously call her "Mother Teresa." May this tireless worker of mercy help us increasingly to understand that our only criterion for action is gratuitous love, free from every ideology and all obligations, offered freely to everyone without distinction of language, culture, race or religion. Mother Teresa loved to say, "Perhaps I don't speak their language, but I can smile." Let us carry her smile in our hearts and give it to those whom we meet along our journey, especially those who suffer. In this way, we will open up opportunities of joy and hope for our many brothers and sisters who are discouraged and who stand in need of understanding and tenderness.

NOTES

1. *Mother Teresa: Come Be My Light: The Private Writings of the "Saint of Calcutta,"* ed. Brian Kolodiejchuk (New York: Doubleday Religion, 2007).

2. See Blaise Pascal, *Pensées,* § 593, trans. A. J. Krailsheimer (New York: Penguin, 1995), 94.

3. Mother Teresa, *Jesus Is My All in All: Praying with the "Saint of Calcutta"* (New York: Doubleday, 2008), 47.

4. John Paul II, *Novo Millennio Ineunte*, [At the Beginning of the New Millennium], 30, http://w2.vatican.va/content/john-paul-ii/en/apost_letters/2001/documents/hf_jp-ii_apl_20010106_novo-millennio-ineunte.html.

5. See Søren Kierkegaard, *Diary*, X, 1, A, 154.

6. Ibid.

7. Mother Teresa, *No Greater Love, Commemorative Edition* (Novarto, CA: New World Library, 2016), 151.

8. *Come Be My Light*, 53.

9. Ibid., 49.

10. Ibid., 49; see also Brian Kolodiejchuk, "A Jesus-centered Life in Response to the Call: Come, Be My Light," *L'Osservatore Romano*, October 19, 2003, 12.

11. See John Paul II, "A Hill in the Land of Moriah," in *The Poetry of John Paul II, Roman Triptych: Meditations*, trans. Jerzy Peterkiewicz (Washington, DC: USCCB Publishing, 2003), 29.

12. Letter to Archbishop Périer, January 13, 1947, in *Come Be My Light*, 48.

13. *Come Be My Light*, 97-98.

14. Ibid., 96.

15. Simone Weil, *Intimations of Christianity among the Ancient Greeks* (New York: Routledge, 1957), 370.

16. John Paul II, *Gift and Mystery* (New York: Image Books, 1999), 12.

17. See St. Caesarius of Arles, "Sermon 223," 1, in *Sermons, Vol. 3*, trans. Sr. Mary Magdeleine Mueller, Fathers of the Church, vol. 66 (Washington, DC: The Catholic University of America Press, 1973), 144; CCL 104.

18. St. Ignatius Loyola, *Spiritual Exercises* (New York: Image Books, 1989), 129-134.

19. John Paul II, "Meditations on the Book of Genesis at the Threshold of the Sistine Chapel," *Roman Triptych*, 25.

20. Prayer for the Thursday after Ash Wednesday.

21. St. Francis of Assisi, "The Legend of Perugia," in *St. Francis of Assisi: Writings and Early Biographies*, ed. Marion A. Habig (Quincy, IL: Franciscan Press, 1972), 1048-1049.

22. St. Francis of Assisi, "Admonitions VI," in *St. Francis of Assisi: Writings*, 81.

23. The documents quoted in this meditation were graciously made available to me by the general postulator of the Cause for Mother Teresa. Some of those that were most personal have subsequently been published in *Come Be My Light*.

24. Dionysius the Areopagite, *The Divine Names*, II, 9, in *Pseudo-Dionysius: The Complete Works*, trans. Paul Rorem (Mahwah, NJ: Paulist Press, 1987), 65.

25. Joseph Neuner, "On Mother Teresa's Charism," *Review for Religious*, vol. 60, no. 5 (September–October 2001): 482.

26. *Come Be My Light*, 169.

27. Johannes Tauler, "Homily 40," *Johannes Tauler: Predigten*, ed. Georg Hofmann (Fribourg: Herder, 1961), 305.

28. See Albert Huart, "Mother Teresa: Joy in the Night," *Review for Religious*, vol. 60, no. 5 (September–October 2001): 494-502.

29. *Come Be My Light*, 177.

30. Ibid., 214.

31. Ibid., 187.

32. Abba Poemen, 37, in *Derwas James Chitty, The Desert a City: An Introduction to the Study of Egyptian and Palestian Monasticism Under the Christian Empire* (Crestwood, NY: St. Vladimir's Seminary Press, 1977), 172; see *Apophtegmata Patrum*, Poemen 37 (PG 65, 332).

33. Henri Martin, "Désolation," in *Dictionnaire de Spiritualité*, vol. 3 (Paris: Beauchesne, 1995), col. 635.

34. St. Paul of the Cross, "Letter to Agnes Grazi" (Letter #116), October 3, 1736, in *The Letters of St. Paul of the Cross*, vol. 1 (Park Ridge, IL: Passionist Provincial Office, 2000), available at www.passiochristi.org.

35. George Varangalakudy, "A Sister for Gandhi," *The Tablet,* October 11, 2003, 12.

36. Padre Pio of Pietrelcina, *Epistolario*, 357, vol. 1, ed. Melchiorre da Pobladura and Alessandro da Ripabottoni (San Giovanni Rotondo: Edizioni "Padre Pio da Pietrelcina," 1973), 817.

37. St. Gregory the Great, *Moralia in Job*, 1, 3, 40 (PL 75, 619).

38. See *Come Be My Light*, 240.

39. Ibid., 194.

40. St. Catherine of Genoa, *Treatise on Purgatory*, 2 (London: Burns and Oates, 1915), 6-8.

41. *Come Be My Light*, 174.

42. See Albert Camus, *The Plague*, trans. Stuart Gilbert (New York: Alfred A. Knopf, 1948), 255.

43. *Come Be My Light*, 192-193.

44. Ibid., 202.

45. Ibid., 198.

46. Letter to the Missionary Sisters of Charity, July 1961, in *Come Be My Light*, 220.

47. Ibid., 230.

48. Karl Rahner, *Concern for the Church,* trans. Edward Quinn, vol. 20, Theological Investigations (New York: Crossroad, 1981), 149.

49. See Augustine, *Confessions,* III, 6, 11, trans. John K. Ryan (New York: Image Books, 1960), 84.

50. Mother Teresa, "Christianity Is Giving," Speech at Cambridge, England, June 10, 1977, in *Speeches That Changed the World*, ed. Simon Sebag Montefiore (London: Quercus, 2005), 191; for a similar interchange on this idea, see *Come Be My Light*, 281.

51. Angela of Foligno, "Instruction XVIII," in *Angela of Foligno: Complete Works*, trans. Paul Lachance (Mahwah, NJ: Paulist Press, 1993), 271.

52. *Come Be My Light*, 238.

53. Abba Arsenius, 27, *Western Asceticism,* ed. Owen Chadwick (Louisville, KY: Westminster John Knox Press, 1958), 91; see also *Apophtegmata Patrum*, from the Coislin manuscript 126, no. 205, ed. François Nau, *Revue de l'Orient Chrétien*, 13 (January 1908): 279.

54. Quoted in *Jesus Is My All in All,* 5.

55. Brian Kolodiejchuk, quoted in *L'Osservatore Romano,*" Special ed., October 19, 2003, 12.

56. "The Varanasi Letter."

57. Ibid.

58. Mother Teresa, *Jesus Is My All in All*, 9.

59. Mother Teresa, Speech to the National Prayer Breakfast, Washington, DC, February 3, 1994, posted on *Crossroads Initiative,* September 2, 2016; for a similar story, see *Come Be My Light*, 281.

60. Phrases from what Mother Teresa called her "business card," *Come Be My Light*, 315.

61. "The Varanasi Letter."

62. Mother Teresa, *Where There Is Love There Is God*, ed. Brian Kolodiejchuk (New York: Doubleday, 2010), 162.

63. Mother Teresa, *In the Heart of the World: Thoughts, Stories and Prayers* (Novato, CA: New World Library, 1997), 33.

64. Mother Teresa, *Jesus Is My All in All*, 9.

65. Comment by Mother Teresa on the topic of "Charity, the Soul of the Mission," Letter to Cardinal Jozef Tomko, January 23, 1991, shared with me by the postulator for her cause.

66. Mother Teresa, Commencement Address to the Class of 1982, St. Thomas Aquinas College, Santa Paula, CA, available at https://thomasaquinas.edu//about/st-teresa-calcutta.

67. Speech to the National Prayer Breakfast.

68. Mother Teresa, *In the Heart of the World: Thoughts, Stories & Prayers*, ed. Becky Benenate (Novato, CA: New World Library, 2010), 45.

69. A photograph of this handwritten prayer, dated on October 9, 1978, is available at https://www.animachristiretreats.org/inspired-by-st-teresa-of-calcutta.html.

70. St. Bonaventure, *The Journey of the Mind to God*, 7, 4, trans. Philotheus Boehner (Indianapolis, IN: Hackett, 1993),38.

71. See Anselm of Canterbury, *Proslogion*, in *Anselm of Canterbury: The Major Works*, ed. Brian Davies and G. R. Evans (Oxford: Oxford University Press, 1998), 82.

72. St. John of the Cross, "Spiritual Canticle" A, stanza 38, in *The Collected Works of St. John of the Cross*, trans. Kieran Kavanaugh and Otilio Rodriguez (Washington, DC: ICS Publications, 2017), 624.

73. See Meister Eckhart, "Sermon One," *The Complete Mystical Works of Meister Eckhart*, trans. and ed. Maurice O'C. Walshe (New York: Crossroad, 2009), 29-37.

74. Origen, "Homily 22," 3, in *Homilies on Luke*, trans. Joseph T. Lienhard, *The Fathers of the Church*, vol. 94 (Washington, DC: The Catholic University of America Press, 1996), p. 93; SCh 87, 302.

75. See Angelus Silesius, *Selections from the "Cherubinic Wanderer,"* 1, 61 (Charleston, SC: BiblioBazaar, 2009), 107: "*Wird Christus tausendmal zu Bethlehem geborn / und nicht in dir: du bleibst noch ewiglich verlorn.*"

76. Giovanni Papini, quoted in Angelo Comastri, *Dov'è il tuo Dio? Storie di conversioni del XX secolo* (Cinisello Balsamo, Italy: San Paolo, 2003), 52.

77. "Mary conceived the Word first in her mind and then in her body." St. Augustine, "Sermon 215," 4, in *The Works of Saint Augustine*, part 3, vol. 6, trans. Edmund Hill, ed. John Rotelle (New Rochelle, NY: New City Press, 1993), 160. See also PL 38, 1074.

78. See what St. Francis of Assisi writes in *Admonitions* 1: "It is really the Spirit of the Lord, Who lives in his faithful, Who receives the most holy body and blood of the Lord."

79. See St. Athanasius of Alexandria, *Life of St. Anthony of Egypt*, 2, trans. Philip Schaff and Henry Wace (N.p.: CreateSpace Publishers, 2016), 6.

80. "The Varanasi Letter."

81. See St. Cyprian of Carthage, *To Quirinus*, II, 20.

82. St. Margaret Mary Alacoque, Third Revelation, June 16, 1675, in *Emile Bougaud, Life of St. Margaret Mary Alacoque* (Charlotte, NC: Tan Books, 1990), 176.

83. See "Message of His Holiness John Paul II for Lent 1993," issued September 18, 1992.

84. "The Varanasi Letter."

85. Pascal, "The Mystery of Jesus," no. 919, in *Pensées*, 289.

86. Thomas of Celano, *Second Life*, 162, 214, in *St. Francis of Assisi: Writings*, 534.

87. Sydney Carter, "Mother Teresa," in *The Lion Christian Poetry Collection*, ed. Mary Batchelor (Oxford: Lion Hudson, 1995), 531.

88. Commentary on the Gospel for the Second Sunday in Lent 2003 for the Program on Rai 1, *A Sua Imagine* ["In His Image"] Recorded at the Missionary Sisters of Charity in Nirmala Kennedy Center, Green Park, Calcutta.

89. First published in 1971; reprinted in 2003 by HarperOne.

90. [Translator's note] Fyodor Dostoevsky, *The Idiot*, III, 5, trans. Henry and Olga Carlisle (New York: New American Library, 1969), 402.

91. [Translator's note] St. Augustine, *Tractates on the First Epistle of John*, 9, 9, trans. John W. Rettig, vol. 92, *The Fathers of the Church* (Washington, DC: The Catholic University of America Press, 1995), 258-259.

92. Commentary on the Gospel for the Second Sunday of Easter, for *A Sua Immagine* [In His Image] on Rai 1, recorded in the year 2000 at the Missionary Sisters of Charity at the Shishu Bhavan House of Calcutta.

93. See Mary Kenny, "Obituary: Mother Teresa of Calcutta," *Independent*, September 7, 1997.

94. [Translator's note] Pascal, *Pensées*, § 919, 314.

95. [Translator's note] G. K. Chesterton, *Heretics* (Nashville, TN: Sam Torode Book Arts, 1906), 133.

96. Delivered at the Meeting with the Families Who Adopted Children from the Sisters of Mother Teresa, on the Third Anniversary of Mother Teresa's Birth in Heaven. Vatican, Paul VI Audience Hall, September 5, 2000.

97. Luke 10:16.

98. Matthew 25:40.

99. See, among others, Eusebius, *Ecclesiastical History*, 6, 2, 11.